Henry Cecil was the pseudonym of Judge Henry Cecil Leon. He was born in Norwood Green Rectory, near London, England in 1902. He studied at Cambridge where he edited an undergraduate magazine and wrote a Footlights May Week production. Called to the bar in 1923, he served with the British Army during the Second World War. While in the Middle East with his battalion he used to entertain the troops with a serial story each evening. This formed the basis of his first book, *Full Circle*. He was appointed a County Court Judge in 1949 and held that position until 1967. The law and the circumstances which surround it were the source of his many novels, plays, and short stories. His books are works of great comic genius with unpredictable twists of plot which highlight the often absurd workings of the English legal system. He died in 1976.

D1490616

BY THE SAME AUTHOR
ALL PUBLISHED BY HOUSE OF STRATUS

SOBER
AS A JUDGE

by

Henry Cecil

HOUSE OF
STRATUS

This edition published in 2000 by House of Stratus, an imprint of
Stratus Books Ltd., 21 Beeching Park, Kelly Bray,
Cornwall, PL17 8QS, UK.
www.houseofstratus.com

Typeset, printed and bound by House of Stratus.

A catalogue record for this book is available from the British Library
and the Library of Congress.

ISBN 1-84232-064-5

Contents

CHAPTER ONE

The New Judge

'Judges in their private lives,' said Henry, 'must not only be good; they must manifestly be seen to be good.'

'Isn't it enough,' said Sally, 'if they're not manifestly seen to be bad?'

'No,' said Henry, 'it is not enough.'

But virtue had no terrors for Roger Thursby, whose appointment to the High Court Bench was being celebrated by himself and his wife and their great friends Henry and Sally Blagrove. In his early days at the Bar Roger had kissed a few girls in taxis and occasionally had a little too much to drink, but his career at the Bar had taken up the rest of his time. Indeed, as a result of his working habits, he had lost – thrown perhaps is the better word – he had thrown Sally to Henry, who had been only too ready to receive her. It all worked out very nicely. Henry was able but lazy and became an excellent County Court judge some years after he had married Sally. Roger went on working and working and, quite by chance, in the middle of work, caught a glimpse of Anne and married her, almost without noticing it. And now he was to have the reward of his labours and to be The Honourable Mr Justice Thursby (professionally) or The Honourable Sir Roger Thursby (privately).

'Tell me,' said Anne, 'why can't Roger be bad now, provided no one knows it?'

'Because,' said Henry, 'there's only one way of ensuring that no one knows it and that's by not doing it. Look at me, I can't even have a drink at the local or people might say I was a pub crawler. And the beer's jolly good there. However, there is one thing you must look out for. Admittedly Roger has no vices, but he has a weakness.'

'And that is?'

'Well, you should know, I'm afraid,' said Henry. 'A tendency to pick up girls in the street.'

'We were both in cars,' said Anne. 'That makes all the difference.'

Roger had, in fact, met Anne through nearly having a collision with her. The collision would have been entirely Anne's fault but Roger had taken the initiative after that.

'For the purpose of argument,' said Roger, 'I am prepared to concede that I picked Anne up in the street. But that single incident does not justify an assault on my moral character as a whole.'

'I never said it was more than a tendency,' said Henry. 'But no one could have walked down Bond Street with Roger on a bright summer day without observing that tendency.'

'Does that mean that, now he's a judge, I can't walk down Bond Street with him any more?' asked Anne. 'It'll be much more expensive for him if I go alone.'

'Surely,' said Roger, 'even a judge is allowed to walk with his eyes open, and to look at the shop windows. And, if a pretty girl happens to get in between, I don't have to blink, do I, or turn the other way?'

'All I can say is,' said Henry, 'that I have seen glances of yours which were anything but judicial, and which, if by mischance photographed and sold to readers of the *Daily*

Jibe, might not look at all well. "Mr Justice Thursby looking round the town," it would be called.'

'Well,' said Roger, 'I hereby give notice that I am not going to change any of my habits. Since I married Anne I have been as good as gold. I pay my rates, I drive with care, I don't bet, I drink, but not to excess, and, if I see an attractive dress or hat, yes – or face under it – I'm going to look at it as much as I like.'

'And now that we've decided that,' said Sally, 'what about next weekend? Are you coming to us or are we coming to you?'

'Well, it can't be next Friday,' said Anne, 'as I've got to go down to father for a few days and I shall only be back on Friday. It'll take me a day to put the house straight after Roger's been on his own for three nights.'

'You think it's safe to leave him after what you've heard from Henry?' said Sally.

'I shall risk it,' said Anne, 'and our daily woman will give me a full report on my return.'

'Well, why not come down to us the week after?' said Henry. 'I tell you what. Let Anne come down in the morning and sit with me in court. You come down later. There's a character I'd like Anne to meet, a Mr Saul Bibury. He's a professional debtor and I can guarantee you your money's worth if he's there. Now, if we're not careful, we shall miss the last train. Good luck to your first case – or perhaps I should say good luck to the poor fellows who appear in front of you.'

Henry and Sally caught their train, while Roger and Anne went back to their London house, and to bed.

'Where are my pyjamas?' called Roger.

Anne opened the bathroom door.

'They're in the airing cupboard, my Lord,' she said, ' – with great respect.'

CHAPTER TWO

The Old Boy

The next day Anne went to Court with Roger to hear his first case. First of all she heard him welcomed on behalf of the Bar by Anthony Trent, QC. Roger had known Trent for a good many years. He had first met him over a case at Westlea, a prosecution for bribery, just at the time he had met Anne. Trent was then a new boy but an incredibly bouncing one, with a self-assurance which nearly drove at least one judge to distraction. But he was extremely able, and, though his appalling self-confidence never left him, as he grew older and more experienced he supplemented it by so much learning and able advocacy that he got on at the Bar very quickly and he had just taken silk when Roger was appointed a judge.

'I can't say', said Trent, 'that I'm sorry that there isn't some more senior member of the Bar to welcome your Lordship to the Bench, because I'm not. Having watched your Lordship grow up and increase in knowledge and stature since I first met your Lordship – when I was in my legal cradle – I feel that there is no one better qualified to speak as to your Lordship's attainments than I am. At the Bar your Lordship was careful, courteous and, if I may say so without disrespect, a good enough lawyer. I'm sure your Lordship will now reveal those additional qualities which the Lord Chancellor must have had in mind when recommending your Lordship for this appointment.'

'Thank you, Mr Trent,' said Roger. 'Thank you very much. May I say that not once since we first met have your speeches ever disappointed me?'

The first case Roger had to try was an accident case. He had done a good many accident cases while he was at the Bar, though they only represented a very small portion of his practice. He had often thought them very unreal. As though the witnesses really knew what happened! As though in many cases the judge could really determine where and in what proportion the blame lay! The whole occurrence was over in a second and it seemed to Roger rather unsatisfactory that whether or not a person, who was seriously injured in an accident, should recover damages should depend on such uncertainties as whether Aunt Hetty (a witness for the plaintiff) or a gentleman in the soft goods trade (a witness for the defendant) really did see the accident and can remember what they saw. And it also seemed rather unfair to Roger that, if you hit the plaintiff hard enough, he almost certainly wouldn't be able to remember what happened. Roger had formed the view that, in cases of personal injury, National Insurance should replace the present hit-or-miss form of judicial enquiry.

'After all,' he said to Henry, 'no one but a lunatic wants to be hurt or killed in a road accident. Why should the injured person's right to damages depend on such imponderables, whether he was careless himself or not?'

However, now that he was a judge, he had to try the cases like any other judge and make the best of it, though he had a feeling that, once he had found his feet, he might from time to time make a suggestion on the subject from the Bench.

His first case took its normal course and eventually counsel for the plaintiff called his independent witness. The witness had only been asked a few questions when counsel on the other side jumped up, protesting hotly that the witness was being asked leading questions.

'I'm sorry,' said the plaintiff's counsel. 'Now, Mr Jones, will you please turn to his Lordship and tell your story in your own way.'

The witness complied.

'Well – it was like this,' he said. 'I was just going for a walk to see my young woman – we'd had a bit of a tiff the night before – you know how these things are – and I was just thinking what I could buy her to sort of make it up – you know what I mean – when I saw old Mrs Higgins on the other side of the road. She and my Dad used to be sweethearts – that was before he met my mother, you'll understand – Mr Higgins is the chemist, or at least he was before he died – they've got a son who carries on the business now – '

At that stage Roger felt that, although he had determined not to open his mouth during a case except to give judgement or unless it was absolutely necessary, there was no alternative to intervening, or the witness might go on until the afternoon without coming to the accident. So he suggested that the witness might say what he actually saw of the collision. It then transpired that Mr Jones had heard a bang, and, looking up, had seen two cars in the middle of the road in an awkward sort of embrace.

Later on the defendant gave his version of the accident and called his independent witness. He was able to give a detailed and graphic account of the accident. He had seen exactly how it all happened. He was watching both cars for several seconds (he called them minutes) before the collision. It was a pretty careful account and quite a credit to the solicitor's clerk who had taken his statement from the witness. But, unfortunately for the defendant, this witness, like the plaintiff's independent witness, had made a statement to the police almost immediately after the accident – in which he said, in almost identical language with that used by the plaintiff's witness: 'I didn't really see anything.' Only, the plaintiff's witness said 'anything', and he said 'nothing'.

Roger eventually decided that each motorist was equally to blame, but on the way home with Anne he confided to her that, although he had conscientiously applied his mind to every word of the evidence and to counsel's speeches, the same result would have been achieved almost equally well by shaking up a lot of dice.

'I thought you did very well,' said Anne, 'and you never once made a joke.'

'I couldn't think of one,' said Roger.

Two days later Anne went to her father but, of course, before doing so, she told Mrs Grain, their daily woman. Mrs Grain had followed Roger's career with interest, and, almost every day from the time when he was appointed, she asked him when he was going to try a murderer.

'Poor Mr Thursby,' she said, ' – Sir Roger I mean, there I go again – what'll I forget next – poor Mr Thursby, having to try one of those, but they're no better than they ought to be or they wouldn't be where they are, would they – which is no more than what they deserve.'

'But they might be innocent,' said Roger.

'Oh, but, Mr Thursby, you wouldn't try them if they were innocent, not you, you wouldn't.'

Roger tried to explain. He felt it desirable that everyone should as far as possible understand the basic principles of English justice. After he had spent some ten minutes on explanation, he said: 'Well, now, Mrs Grain, do you understand that?'

'Oh – yes, Mr Thursby, you make it ever so clear. But, all the same, you wouldn't try the innocent ones, not you, you wouldn't. It wouldn't be right, would it, not if they hadn't done anything.'

Roger gave it up as a bad job.

'What'll you do tonight?' asked Anne.

'I'll go to the club, I expect,' said Roger.

'You won't be lonely?'

'Of course I shall. That's what you want, isn't it?' They kissed, and Roger left for Court.

He walked all the way. He was very happy. He knew that he would find his new job very satisfying and within his ability. And now he would have so much more time to be with Anne, whom he adored. Now they'd be able to go to concerts and theatres together. Life begins at forty-six. It took him three quarters of an hour to walk, but it seemed only a few minutes. He went through the judges' entrance and straight to his room. His clerk was waiting for him.

'D'you know anything about nylon stockings, sir?' he asked.

'Only that they're expensive and don't last. No, I don't really.'

'Well, you will, sir. The first case. I fancy they're going to invite you to see a demonstration. Where'll you have it, in here?'

'I shouldn't think so,' said Roger. 'If I clutter up the judges' corridor with young ladies showing off their nylons in my first week, I shan't be popular.'

'That's what *you* think, sir. I can't see any objections being raised. But I'm sorry to disappoint you, sir – the demonstration's going to be on a machine.'

'Then why on earth did you ask if I'd have it in here?'

'Just to see the reaction, sir. I think that's your usher –
excuse me, sir.'

The clerk left and came back in a moment or two and
helped Roger to put on his robes. Then the usher led him
to his court, and he went in, bowed to counsel, and sat
down. The visions which the mention of nylon stockings
is liable to conjure up in many men's minds soon
disappeared when the case was opened. It was obvious
that it would be a highly technical case about gauges and
deniers and even more esoteric terms, and that Roger
would learn something about the way nylon stockings
were made – but not how they were put on or what they
looked like in position.

The case was not over when Roger rose at the end of the
day and went to his room to disrobe. He was a little
disappointed that Anne had gone to her father. Still, an
evening at the club would be very pleasant.

Then his clerk informed him that a Major Plumstead
wanted to see him. A purely personal matter.

Plumstead, thought Roger, Plumstead? But it can't be.
Roger had been at school with a boy called Plumstead, and
they had formed a rather odd combination. Roger, rather a
prig, very disinclined to break any of the school rules and
horribly inclined to admit the offence if he did. Plumstead,
a wild scapegrace with all the worst schoolboy instincts –
never telling the truth when a lie would serve as well,
breaking every rule within reach and even some beyond it,
flouting authority for the sake of doing so and brazenly
denying his fault right up to the last moment. It had
certainly been a queer friendship and had from time to
time landed Roger in trouble. Plummer, as they called him,
never tried to get Roger out of a scrape, though he never
threw the blame on him unnecessarily. 'Each man for
himself' was the motto, and no complaints, whatever

happened. It was probably the attraction of opposites. The anarchist in Plummer had a fascination for Roger, while Plummer could not resist Roger's virtuous instincts. Their partnership worked well, too, on the football field, where Plummer was scrum half and Roger fly. They knew each other's game perfectly, and would execute some extremely effective, if unorthodox, movements, which were usually a feature of any game in which they were playing. Indeed, when there was an issue as to whether one or other of them should be kept in as a punishment, any master concerned either kept them both in or neither. With the result that, if a school match was involved, Plummer could do almost what he liked, knowing that the virtuous Roger would do nothing. Indeed, it was partly the sight of Roger, sitting primly at his desk, not talking to his neighbour when the master had gone outside for a moment, because they had been forbidden to talk, that brought out the devil in Plummer. And Roger would make things even worse because, if he were compelled to break the order so as not to be too rude to his neighbour, he would solemnly confess his fault, if, on returning, the master asked if anyone had spoken. And the crowning anguish for Plummer was when Roger refused to say to whom he had been talking, lest he should get the real culprit into trouble. On one such occasion he said quietly to himself: 'The boy stood on the burning deck.'

'Did you say something, Plumstead?' asked the master.

'No, sir,' said Plummer. 'It was my thoughts you must have heard, sir. They must have been very loud, sir. Thoughts can be heard, sir, you know. That's why one has to be so careful, sir. As a matter of fact, sir, I heard what you were thinking the other day, sir. You were – '

'Shut up, Plumstead,' said the master. There was a school match on that day.

Plumstead left school before Roger and made the Army his career. Although they met once or twice afterwards, they soon drifted apart and Roger had not seen or heard of his friend for over twenty years when his arrival was announced. He told his clerk to show him in and wondered what change the years would prove to have made. He could not know that mentally there was hardly any change at all.

'Major Plumstead, sir,' said the clerk, and Plummer burst into the room.

'My dear old lordship,' he said.

'Plummer,' said Roger.

The clerk went out and for a split second – just time enough for the normal accident – they simply looked at one another.

'Where have I been all these years?' said Plummer eventually. 'Go on, ask me that. I've known where you've been. Watched your career with interest and approval. For the plaintiff Mr Thursby, for the defendant Mr Thursby, QC, the judge is Mr Justice Thursby. Good for you, old boy. Only goes to show. Virtue pays. Look at me. Just a major. And out on my ear at that. Not court-martialled, old boy. Just axed. No, I haven't come looking for a job. Don't look so anxious. And I don't want a loan, either. Just come to see whether success has spoiled you. 'Fraid it won't have. Nothing could spoil you. Too good to be true. Well, how are you, old boy, after all this time?'

'Well,' said Roger, 'it's nice to see you, Plummer.'

Plummer exploded with laughter.

'What's the joke?' said Roger.

Plummer exploded again and then, gasping for breath, looked at Roger, his eyes mutely appealing for help.

'Don't, old boy,' he said. 'It's impossible.'

He recovered after a moment or two.

'What is it?' asked Roger. 'Have I said something?'

'Don't speak,' said Plummer, 'or I'll have apoplexy. Write it down. Oh – my wig and toenails,' and he had a further paroxysm.

'Sorry, old boy,' he said, when he had finally subsided, 'but you're so the same. You haven't changed, that's the trouble. You're just the same horrible, good, literal-minded little boy that I couldn't get away from in the Lower Fourth.' He paused. 'Oh, good Lord,' he said suddenly, 'is this contempt of court?'

'Sorry to disappoint you,' said Roger. 'I'm afraid it isn't. You can say what you like to a judge privately, so long as it isn't about a case, or his behaviour in Court.'

'You don't say,' said Plummer. 'You don't really say. Oh dear, I'm sorry. Here we go again,' and he had another outburst.

'Well, how have things gone with you – apart from the Army I mean,' said Roger eventually. 'Are you married? Any children? Where do you live, and so on?'

'I'm not exactly married,' said Plummer. 'Had a divorce, I'm afraid. Nothing bad, you know. It was all arranged as a matter of fact. We couldn't stand each other. Still, I suppose I oughtn't to tell you all this. What about you?'

Roger told him.

'Any chance of seeing Anne?' asked Plummer. 'I'd love to see who had to put up with you for life.'

'I'd have taken you home tonight,' said Roger, 'but unfortunately Anne's down at Westlea with her father. Are you going to be in London for long?'

'All depends, old boy. I might be. Anyway, I shall be back again soon. What are you doing tonight?'

'Nothing, as a matter of fact.'

'How about dinner, then, and a show, perhaps?'

'Good idea.'

Plummer thought for a moment.

'No – I tell you what. I've got a little cottage about forty miles from London. Get your toothbrush and come and spend the night. I'll tell you some of my misdeeds in the past twenty years – show you some too, perhaps. It's a bit primitive, but we've got water and electric light and all that. What d'you say? I've got a car outside. Take you round to your place and then off we go. Done?'

'Done,' said Roger. 'I'll just ring Anne and tell her. What's the address, and are you on the telephone?'

'That's right,' said Plummer, 'tell Mummy. Oh dear, oh dear, oh dear.'

Shortly afterwards they left the Law Courts and drove to Roger's house. Plummer certainly had a car outside the Law Courts. It was a large sports car, painted bright red. Its number was – IMA I.

'Had to pay five pounds for that,' explained Plummer. 'Makes it easy for the police to pick me up.'

When they reached Roger's house they went in to have a drink, and Roger told Mrs Grain that he would be away for the night.

'Oh, Mr Thursby,' said Mrs Grain, 'will you be trying that murderer on Monday – the one what drowned his wife in soapsuds? Oh, it was terrible. I know what I'd do with him. He couldn't even just use ordinary water. Even that Mr Smith who drowned all his wives, until they stopped him, only used water. But soapsuds – it don't seem right.'

'No,' said Roger, 'it's wrong.'

'You won't let him do it again, will you, sir – not with soapsuds.'

'Well, I'm not taking the case, Mrs Grain,' said Roger, 'otherwise I'd certainly tell him, if he were let off, that in future soapsuds were out.'

'I believe you said that just to please me, sir,' said Mrs Grain. 'But I lie awake sometimes at night thinking of these terrible things. Just think if Mr Grain had thought of doing it to me. But he wouldn't have, not with soapsuds he wouldn't. He was that kind was Mr Grain.'

Having satisfied Mrs Grain as best he could, Roger telephoned Anne and told her where he would be. They dined at Roger's club, where Plummer made a telephone call, and then they set off.

If Roger had realized what the journey was going to be like he would have unhesitatingly refused the invitation. Plummer began by trying to go the wrong way round Trafalgar Square.

'So sorree, officer,' he said, in a faked foreign accent. 'We from Brazil. My friend he no speak Eenglish at all. I speakee not too good. Please to excuse. I go proper way now.'

And he roared off down the Mall at fifty miles an hour.

'I say, Plummer,' said Roger, 'there's a limit of thirty here.'

'Speedo's wrong, old boy. Registers twenty too much. You'll see, when we're on the open road.'

Roger froze to his seat, thinking of the open road. But what could he do? It would be horribly rude to ask to be allowed to get out and go home. And, even if he did, Plummer would probably refuse and drive all the faster. Indeed, he ought to have thought of that before. Plummer loved baiting. The more one appeared to be worried by his antics the more Plummer would indulge in them. He must be quite nonchalant – try to pretend they were the normal thing. Even so he couldn't avoid wincing when they dashed across the lights at Grosvenor Place.

'Sorry, old boy,' said Plummer. 'Colour blind.'

'Then how did you know they were red?' asked Roger.

'Don't,' said Plummer, 'or we'll have an accident.'

Somehow or other they got through London without being stopped by the police. Beneath the mask of nonchalance which Roger was trying, not too successfully, to wear, he was thinking anxiously what he would say if in fact they were stopped, and he himself were questioned. Eventually he could restrain himself no longer: 'Look, old boy,' he said, 'I wish you'd drive a bit slower. I dare say it sounds silly to you but it wouldn't be a good thing for me to be involved in an accident.'

'Sorry, old boy,' said Plummer, 'is that better?' and he put his foot even harder on the accelerator.

At last they came to a halt. Not entirely voluntarily. They were going through a small village where there was a pedestrian crossing. Just in time Plummer saw an old woman starting to cross one side and a couple of children the other. By some extremely skilful driving Plummer avoided them all and ended up by half uprooting the post with the flashing beacon on it.

'Near thing,' he said to Roger, as he drew away from the beacon, and drove off as fast as possible. 'Fortunately one's too old, and the others are too young to get my number.'

'But aren't you going to report it?' said Roger.

'Don't,' said Plummer, 'please don't or we'll have something really bad.'

'Now look,' said Roger sternly, 'I'm sorry to be difficult about this but you must report it, really you must. I don't even mind sharing the cost of the damage with you.'

'Look, old boy,' said Plummer. 'Will you say you were driving?' and he laughed so loudly that he had to slow down slightly.

'I'm awfully sorry,' said Roger, 'I know it's terribly funny to you and you think I'm a dreadful prig and all that. Well – I am, if you like, but, if you don't report it, I shall have to. We're not at school any longer.'

'Of course I shall report it, old boy,' said Plummer, 'but shall I say you were with me?'

'Of course,' said Roger stiffly.

'I won't if you'd rather not,' said Plummer.

'Naturally you must, if they ask you,' said Roger.

'But suppose they don't, old boy, shall I volunteer it?'

'You must volunteer it, if you think fit,' said Roger.

'Sorry you're so touchy, old boy,' said Plummer. 'If you're like this now – ' He paused.

'Yes?' said Roger.

'Nothing, old boy. I was just wondering what you'd be like if we had a real accident.'

'I should probably be dead,' said Roger.

They drove in silence for a while. Then: 'I hope you're not sorry you came, old boy?' said Plummer.

Roger said nothing.

'You'll feel better when we get there. I'll mix you something special,' went on Plummer.

Roger smiled.

'You used to say the same sort of thing at school. D'you remember that box of chocolates you promised me if I'd let you in the dorm window?'

'Don't tell me I never gave it to you. Here, let me feel – '

He took both hands off the wheel and started to feel in his pockets.

'I don't want it as badly as that,' said Roger hurriedly. 'I say – look out – '

The remark was forced out of Roger. Plummer had gone the wrong way round a roundabout, missed a cycle, gone on to the kerb, back to the road and then on to the pavement on the wrong side of the road to avoid an oncoming car and then back to the road again.

'She's a beauty to handle, isn't she?' said Plummer. 'But you were saying something – '

'If I was,' said Roger, 'it'll wait till my heart's beating again. I'm not as young as I was thirty years ago.'

'Is it only that? Then you can't be more than forty-six. Young for a judge, isn't it?'

'They make them younger than they used to. And I was lucky.'

'Hope it holds out, old boy,' said Plummer, as he pressed on.

Twenty minutes later they drove through some gates and up a long drive leading to a low Georgian house.

'What's this?' said Roger.

'Welcome,' said Plummer.

'But you said it was a cottage.'

'Just modesty, old boy.'

'You must have done well for yourself.'

'Oh, not so bad, old boy.'

'You didn't get this out of the Army.'

'You've said it, old boy. I certainly didn't. Fortunately, I've had a sideline or two. Come in.'

He led Roger into the house and took him to the library. 'This'll suit you best,' said Plummer. 'No law reports, I'm afraid, but some good, sound, boring English literature. I'll fetch the drinks. Sit down and make yourself at home.'

Plummer went out and Roger, after glancing at the books, picked one out and sat down. He started to read but, after a few minutes, he fell lightly asleep. The strain of the drive had had its effect.

He was woken up by two cool hands being placed on his eyes. They were obviously not Plummer's.

'Hello, sugar,' said a young female voice with a spurious American accent. 'Where have you been hiding yourself?'

Roger suddenly remembered Plummer's remark: 'If you're like this now ...' and the pause at the end of it. The cool hands were still on his eyes. He had to do or say something.

'How d'you do?' he said.

'How does who do?' said the voice.

'I've no idea, I'm afraid.'

'Well, guess.'

'I think there's some mistake,' said Roger. 'I'm sure I don't know you.'

'Well, I know you, sugar. Go on, guess.'

'But I've really no idea. You're a friend of Plummer's, I suppose.'

'Who's he?'

'Our host.'

'Oh, him. More a friend of yours than mine, sugar.'

'Do please take your hands away,' said Roger. 'I'm sure there's a mistake.'

'You sound as though you wanted it to be a mistake.'

'Look,' said Roger, removing the cool hands with his, as gently as he could, 'I'm very sorry but I've never seen you before in my life.'

He said that as he got his first look at the girl. And he knew it must be true. He would never have forgotten a face like that in a hurry. It was more attractive than beautiful, but whatever you called it, it wasn't a face to forget.

'You're kidding,' she said. 'Remember the Soft Shoe Club?'

'I've never heard of it,' said Roger.

18

'Were you as blind as all that? You talked sober enough.'

'I tell you I've never heard of the Soft or any other Shoe Club in my life and I've never been there and I've never met you before.'

'Well, how d'you do, then, honey?' said the girl. 'It must have been some other handsome guy. I'm sorry. Anyway, we've met now. I'm Toni.'

'How d'you do?' said Roger, again wondering how long Plummer was going to be and then realizing he was very likely enjoying the scene through a peephole.

'And who are you, handsome, seeing that you're not the other guy?'

'I'm Roger Thursby,' he said after a pause.

'That's all right,' said Toni. 'You don't have to apologize. It's a nice name. I love Roger.'

Well, thank heaven she doesn't know who I am, thought Roger. That's something, anyway.

At that moment the young woman sat on his knee and Plummer walked in.

'Oh,' he said, 'I see you know each other.'

'Look – ' said Roger.

'I am,' said Plummer. 'You seem to have fixed yourself up all right. I didn't exactly mean that when I said "make yourself at home", but don't move, it's quite OK. But you might introduce me.'

For answer Roger lifted up the lady, plumped her down on the settee and turned on Plummer.

'Look here. What is this?' he said. 'I don't know this young woman from Adam – '

'Eve, you mean,' said Plummer.

'Where is the nearest station?' said Roger. 'I'm leaving.'

'Good ten miles' walk, I'm afraid.'

'Will you kindly drive me there?'

'It wouldn't be any use if I did. Last train will have gone.'

'I'll go to an hotel then.'

'I can't recommend any.'

'I don't want your recommendation,' said Roger angrily.

'Well, there's a pub which has a bed or two five miles away but they'll be in bed now and won't thank you for knocking them up.'

'I do hope you're not leaving on my account,' said the girl. 'Have I done anything? Most men like it.' She draped herself over one of the chairs. Even one of Her Majesty's judges could not help observing that it was a most attractive sight.

'I'm sorry,' said Roger. 'There's obviously been some misunderstanding. I was a fool not to have thought of it.'

'All right,' said Plummer, 'I'll explain in a moment or two. There's nothing to it really. When you said you'd come, I just telephoned Toni to come down with her sister. She'll be here in a moment. They won't manhandle you any more, I promise. I'll call them off. Toni – you're to leave the gentleman alone.'

'Usually,' said Toni, 'the warning's the other way round.'

'Usually,' said Plummer, 'we don't have the honour of entertaining one of Her Majesty's judges. Their self-control is horrible to see. Let me present Sir Roger Thursby. Miss Toni Mandeville. Her real name is Dora Stokes but we thought the other was more impressive.'

'How d'you do?' said Roger.

'Toni and Gillian are at the Soft Shoe Club. They're hostesses.'

'Oh,' said Roger.

'I have an interest there,' said Plummer. 'One of my sidelines. I don't suppose you'll want to visit us. Although we're highly respectable, I assure you. Duchesses come to us. You could bring your wife one day.'

'Thanks,' said Roger, 'I'll think about it.'

'I've never sat on a High Court Judge's knee before,' said Toni.

'It'll be useful experience,' said Plummer. 'You might be called to do so as a demonstration. I see that a judge had a cabaret show or something given specially the other day to prove something or other.'

'In the most unlikely event of something of the kind being necessary,' said Roger, 'I should call the usher.'

'What a waste,' said Plummer. 'Now, will you forgive me a moment while I go and see what Gillian's doing? I guarantee your safety with Toni.'

'Oh, very well,' said Roger, and Plummer went out.

'Well,' said Toni, 'now what?'

Roger said nothing.

'Don't look so unhappy,' said Toni. 'I know you're a judge, but that isn't everything, is it? I couldn't do your job, but you couldn't do mine.'

'That's true,' said Roger. 'Quite frankly, I'm not sure that I'd want to.'

'That goes for me too,' said Toni. 'Sitting up there all day being stuffy, and then being stuffy all over again when you step down. Wouldn't suit me at all. Don't you ever let your back hair down?'

'If I had any, I'm not sure that I would,' said Roger.

'You must be miserable. Don't you ever have any fun?'

'Of course we do.'

'It all depends what you call fun,' said Toni. 'You don't look so old and you're quite good-looking, but if there were a prize for misery I'd give it to you. D'you mind my talking like this?'

'Would it make any difference if I did?' asked Roger.

'It might,' said Toni. 'I'm quite kind. I'd be terrified of you in Court with your wig and things, but now you look just a poor, unhappy little man. I'd love to cheer you up.'

'How?' said Roger.

'That's better,' said Toni, 'that's the first sign of life. Well, you can give me a kiss if you like, just to show there's no ill feeling.'

Roger thought for a moment, and before he had time to answer, Toni went on: 'This is a great experience,' she said. 'I can see you trying out the question whether you'll kiss me or not, like you'd try a case. On the one hand, you say to yourself – she's a pretty girl and it'd be rather nice, and, on the other hand, I'm a judge and I didn't ought. That's right, isn't it?'

Roger laughed.

'You should have gone to the Bar,' he said.

'Well – what is the verdict?'

'For the defendant, I'm afraid,' said Roger.

'Who's that?' said Toni.

'Me,' said Roger.

'That means you win, I suppose?' said Toni.

'Yes,' said Roger.

'OK,' said Toni, and came up and kissed him full on the mouth.

'By winning I meant,' said Roger, when she had finished, 'that I didn't kiss you.'

'That's not very polite,' said Toni. 'Anyway, now you've had it both ways. Did you like it?' she added.

'I don't feel called upon to answer that question,' said Roger.

'What happens if a witness refuses to answer in Court?' asked Toni.

'That depends,' said Roger. 'If it's a question he's bound to answer I can fine him or send him to prison.'

'It's not the same here,' said Toni. 'He just gets kissed again.'

Roger got up and backed away.

'No,' he said. 'I'm sorry. It just can't be done.'

'It has been,' said Toni.

'Look,' said Roger, 'you strike me, if I may say so without offence, as a very intelligent girl. Why don't you do something other than being a dance hostess?'

'Such as?'

'Secretary to a doctor or something.'

'Shouldn't get paid enough. I want to cash in on my good looks while I get the chance. I can't model or act – this is about the only thing. And it's quite fun. More than with a doctor. I should know – my father's one.'

'Well,' said Roger, 'you know your own business best, but you're very young and if you should change your mind, I – that is, my wife and I – might be able to help. We know a doctor or two.'

'How sweet of you,' she said. 'You must be an understanding judge. If ever I'm up for anything I'd like to be in front of you. Now, don't be frightened,' she added, and she came up and kissed him lightly on the forehead.

Although Roger's behaviour was neither bad nor manifestly seen to be bad, it gave him rather a shock to think that within a few days of his becoming a judge he had been kissed by a pretty stranger and had had her on his knee. But she certainly was a very pretty stranger – very, very pretty. Perhaps there was something in what Henry had said about him after all. He remembered saying to Sally many, many years previously: 'Girls have a tremendous

23

fascination for me. And, if one of them has sort of been in my arms, it does things to me afterwards. I go on thinking about it. It multiplies.' Well, Toni had most certainly not been in his arms but – oh, well, there was nothing else he could have done about it.

Plummer returned a moment later.

'How are we doing?' he asked.

'My judge is doing very well,' said Toni. 'You'd hardly know he was one.'

'Good,' said Plummer. 'He must be improving. But you look remarkably tidy. That suggests there's still a good bit of judge in him. But Rome wasn't built in a day. If you say he's doing well, then there must be hope for him yet.'

'Would you very much mind telling me what all this is about?' asked Roger.

'That's fair enough,' said Plummer. 'Drink this, and I'll explain.'

He handed Roger a cocktail. Then he began. 'D'you remember', he said, 'when a man dug up Piccadilly, and it was quite a long time before they found it was a hoax?'

'I've heard of it,' said Roger.

'Well, that wasn't me,' said Plummer.

'I see,' said Roger. 'Where does that lead me to?'

'It wasn't me,' said Plummer, 'but it might have been. Whenever I'm bored, I do something like that.'

'Well?' said Roger.

'I was bored this morning,' said Plummer, 'and I suddenly remembered the horrible little boy who'd been made a judge.'

'You mean', said Roger, 'that you like making fools of people and generally upsetting them.'

'That's right,' said Plummer. 'Particularly their dignity. D'you remember Measles?'

He was referring to a pimply boy who had been at school with them.

Roger thought. 'Yes, he's a general now, or something?'

'That's right.'

'What about him?'

'He's just the same. In looks, I mean. Pompous now, though. I took him for a ride.'

'You've never grown up, Plummer,' said Roger.

'No, thank God,' said Plummer, 'and I don't propose to.'

'How did he like it here?'

'Oh, I didn't bring him down here. He'd have enjoyed the trip and loved the girls. Plenty of fun for him. None for me. No, I have other ways with generals. D'you remember Trundle?'

'The Bishop?'

'Well, he's one now. Yes, that's him. I gave him a demonstration, too.'

'As far as I can see,' said Roger, 'you spend your time and money on trying to annoy boys who were at school with you.'

'Oh – I don't limit it to them. There aren't enough who are worthwhile. I shouldn't have touched you, if you hadn't been a judge.'

'May I take it', said Roger, 'that you've now relieved your boredom and I'm finished with?'

'Part one,' said Plummer. 'Part two will *not* follow immediately.'

'That's something,' said Roger.

'But it will follow,' said Plummer. 'Another drink?'

CHAPTER THREE

Plummer in Court

There were no further incidents that night, and the next morning Plummer drove Roger to the Law Courts. Roger nearly telephoned Anne from his room, but decided that it would be better to say what he wanted to from home. His clerk informed him that he had another running-down case to try and he was quite glad to have the chance of taking his mind off Plummer and Toni. But he was not able to do so for long, for there in the well of the Court sat Plummer.

Theoretically the well of the Court is meant for witnesses, barristers and solicitors, and their clients, and not for sightseers, for whom there is a gallery. But, unless a court is very crowded, anyone who wishes will be allowed to sit in the well of the Court. In these circumstances Roger did not feel that he should send an usher to turn Plummer out. If he did, Plummer would only go up to the gallery and look from there. Of course, if he misbehaved, he would have to be turned out or fined or even sent to prison for contempt of court. But Roger didn't like the idea of doing anything like that at all. For all Plummer's eccentricity, he still liked the boy. That was really how he still thought of him. But what was this boy now going to do? At school he was capable of doing anything.

Roger soon found out. Every time Roger said anything, Plummer gave the faintest nod or shake of the head, indicating agreement or disagreement with Roger's observation. The movement was so slight that, unless carefully observed by someone on the lookout for it, it would not be noticed, and it was so slight that, if a complaint were made, Plummer could say with a look of innocence – which Roger knew so well: 'I'm so sorry. I was quite unaware of it. Please convey my apologies to his Lordship. One moment, usher, perhaps I have a tic and don't know it.'

It was obvious that, unless Roger took action, no one else would, and in all the circumstances Roger felt that the best course was to ignore it. But, in the same way that it is very difficult to keep one's eyes away from a particularly ugly object or person, Plummer's nods and shakes had a fatal fascination for Roger.

The accident case was not quite the normal type. For this was the case of a hit-and-run driver. Almost every driver stops after an accident, but this defendant was an exception. Normally there would have been no litigation, as the insurance company would have paid up, accepting their insured's flight as satisfactory evidence that he was in the wrong. But two things prevented that course from being taken. First, the damages which would be recovered, if the plaintiff won, would be very high indeed, and secondly, in spite of the defendant's bad behaviour in driving on, it certainly looked as though the accident might, in part at least, have been due to the negligence of the plaintiff himself.

In order to support this plea the defendant called his passenger to corroborate his evidence. Part of the cross-examination of this witness was as follows:

COUNSEL: Are you a truthful person, Mr Smith?

SMITH: As much as most.

COUNSEL: Or do you mean as little?

SMITH: That's for you to say.

COUNSEL: Then you don't always tell the truth?

SMITH: No, not always. Nor does anyone.

ROGER: Don't make statements. Just answer the questions, please.

(*Plummer gave a slight nod of approval.*)

COUNSEL: You've given evidence today which, if true, would show that your friend the defendant was in no way to blame for the accident, haven't you?

SMITH: Yes.

COUNSEL: But shortly after the accident you told a very different story to the police, didn't you?

SMITH: Have I got to answer that?

ROGER: Certainly you have.

(*Again Plummer nodded.*)

SMITH: Well – yes, I did.

COUNSEL: You told them, didn't you, that you'd come by an altogether different route, and hadn't been involved in an accident at all?

SMITH: Something of the sort.

COUNSEL: Why?

SMITH: Because my friend had said so, and I had to back him up when the police asked me.

COUNSEL: Let me understand this. Are you saying that shortly after the accident your friend was asked for his account of it by the police, and that he lied about it?

SMITH: He said he hadn't had an accident.

COUNSEL: He lied about it?

SMITH: Well, if you put it that way – yes.

COUNSEL: Is there any other way to put it?

(*No answer.*)

COUNSEL: Well, now you say, do you not, that later the police came to see you?

SMITH: Yes.

COUNSEL: And you knew that your friend had lied about it?

SMITH: That he'd said he hadn't been in an accident – yes.

COUNSEL: That he'd lied about it?

SMITH: Well – yes.

COUNSEL: And so you lied about it, too?

SMITH: Well – I said –

COUNSEL: Never mind what you said – you lied about it?

SMITH: I suppose I did.

COUNSEL: You lied to the police?

SMITH: Yes.

ROGER: Of course, while no one can approve of telling lies to the police, there's no doubt the witness had a conflict of loyalties – which one can sympathize with (*Plummer nodded*) – if not condone (*Plummer shook his head*).

COUNSEL: With respect, my Lord, it was the passenger's duty to report the matter to the police in any event.

ROGER: Is that so? You may be right – shall we go on with the evidence?

(*Plummer nodded.*)

In the end Roger decided that both parties were equally to blame, and on his way home he again reflected that he might have produced as good a result with the toss of a coin. As soon as he was home he telephoned Anne.

'Do you think you could come back tomorrow?' he said.

'Why? Anything particular?'

'No, not really – but I think it would be nice if you could manage it.'

'Well, I'm not sure,' said Anne.

'A lovely girl has been sitting on my knee,' said Roger.

'What did you say?' said Anne.

Roger repeated his remark.

'I'll come,' said Anne.

CHAPTER FOUR

Hotel de Luxe

That night, after he had described his adventures to Anne, Roger spent a little time before going to sleep in asking himself whether he could have done anything else as far as Plummer was concerned. He ought, he supposed, to have jumped out of the car at Trafalgar Square, when Plummer's behaviour and his knowledge of Plummer should have warned him that worse might be in store. After that he never had a chance until they had hit the beacon post. And, if he'd insisted on leaving in the few seconds' opportunity he had then, he would have had to go to a police station and report the matter. It was true that he was no longer at school but it would have been a very difficult duty to discharge. No, it was better to have let the few seconds go – no one could blame him for that – and to be swept on by the inexorable Plummer. As for Toni – well, as for Toni – yes, it was a nicer name than Dora – as for Toni – she certainly was an attractive girl – yes, of course, there was, he supposed, too much sentimentality about girls who go wrong – which reminded him of Plummer's remark about a girl who, he said, had gone pleasantly wrong during the war – too much sentimentality, yes, perhaps, but that shouldn't stop one from lending a helping hand when needed – thank heaven he had a

31

sensible wife like Anne – she understood – they could help Toni together – she ought to marry some nice young man – a barrister, perhaps – they could ask one or two to drinks – that would mean Toni coming to the house quite often – well, Annie wouldn't mind that – and she was incredibly attractive – but it was a shame that she was in a club – perhaps Anne could do something – Anne was a wonderful wife – Anne – Toni – Anne – Toni – and he fell asleep. Into his dreams appeared the Lord Chief Justice: 'What's this I hear, Thursby?' he said.

'I'm sorry, Chief, she just sat down and I couldn't get her off.'

'I always use a pin myself,' said the Chief, and vanished. The rest of Roger's night was uneventful, apart from one moment when he murmured 'Toni', and another when Anne kicked him.

The next morning she went with Roger to Court. In the Strand a man came up to them.

'Filthy postcard?' he said. 'View of the Law Courts.' It was Plummer.

After they had disentangled themselves from him, Roger took Anne to his room, and asked the clerk to bring the papers in the first case.

'I'll give you an idea of what it's about. Make it easier to follow. You often miss a good deal from the back of the Court.'

The clerk brought the papers and Roger looked at them.

'Good,' he said, after a moment. 'You should enjoy this. It's about an hotel. A chap is suing for damages on the ground that it didn't come up to expectations.'

'I'm glad someone's got the nerve,' said Anne. 'I hope he wins. English hotels are the end.'

'Not all,' said Roger, 'but a good one does take a bit of finding. But you mustn't start prejudicing me with your views, or people will say it's your decision, not mine.'

He sent Anne into Court and not long afterwards went in himself.

'This action,' began Anthony Trent, in opening the case, 'well illustrates the forbearance of the English people. They put up with almost anything in the way of discomfort, discourtesy, and bad food in English hotels.'

'Hear, hear,' said Anne very quietly to herself.

'They occasionally grouse,' went on Counsel, 'they occasionally go a bit red in the face when they have been kept waiting three quarters of an hour for lunch and are then told that everything is off except cottage pie and prunes and rice, and they occasionally swear when the hot water is cold. But, as for bringing an action for breach of contract – well, it is hardly ever heard of. The average man prefers to swallow the inferior coffee, stub his toes on the end of the too-small bed or on his wife (preferably the latter) and eat the mixture of milk powder and egg with an anchovy on top and a soggy mess of bread below, described in the high sounding menu as *Canapé Ecossais* – rather than risk litigation. And, as long as people will put up with what they are given, they will not be given better.

'Every now and then, however, a pioneer emerges, someone who is prepared to litigate and not count the cost, someone for whom the culinary and other insults, compared with the language on the brochure, prove too much. And my client, Mr de Blame (it is pronounced like the ordinary word, my Lord), my client is one of them.

'Last summer he was sent a brochure by the defendants, who are the owners of the Grand Hotel at Snortingbury-on-Sea. The material parts of this document I will now read to your Lordship: "This is *par excellence* the hotel *de luxe* in the South of England. Here is combined superb food with gracious living in the old style. Here you will find the food fit for gourmets of international reputation and the service something which you have not experienced anywhere in this country since the war. Ask the chef for *Oeufs Américains à l'Orgueil*. Families specially catered for. Quiet room for those who want it, playroom for the young, television-room for all and sundry. Our terms are not low but every farthing is returned to you with interest in the happiness which we take pleasure in providing for you. Mr and Mrs Sweep, resident proprietors."

'The defendants did not explain', went on Counsel, 'how every farthing could be returned and the resident proprietors still survive, let alone how they could afford to pay interest as well. But my client, who wanted a holiday and had too often gone to hotels on other people's recommendations, replied to the letter which enclosed the brochure, as follows: "Dear Sir: If your hotel is really substantially in accordance with what you represent it to be, I should like a double room and private bathroom for myself and my wife for fourteen days from the 1st August. I need good food, quiet, and comfort, and am prepared to pay for it."

'Mr Sweep replied that he would be delighted to accommodate my client at the inclusive charge of forty-five guineas per week, and, in consequence, they arrived at the hotel on the 1st August. They left on the 3rd and issued a writ on the 1st September. My client claims that he was entitled to leave. He says that the statements made in the brochure were false and that he was compelled to take a suite of rooms at a large hotel elsewhere, as that was the only accommodation available in the first fortnight of August. He claims the difference in cost, which was considerable, and a further sum as damages for the discomfort he suffered during his forty-eight hours at the Grand Hotel, Snortingbury, and for the inconvenience in having to move.'

Trent was right in describing his client as a litigant who did not count the cost. He had made this plain at the outset: 'I don't mind about money,' he had told his solicitor, 'but I won't be cheated. Bring them to their knees. Don't settle on any account. Don't hesitate to get in touch with me, whenever you want me. When you want money, ask for it.'

The solicitor briefed Trent as leader. He explained to his client that Trent was a bit irritating but that he knew his job as well as anybody.

'In what way irritating?'

'You'll see in conference,' the solicitor had said. And Mr de Blame did see. But, as he completely trusted his solicitor's good judgement, he accepted Trent's insufferable condescension with equanimity.

'I should have thought', Trent had said, 'that a gentleman of your experience would have known better than to fall for a brochure like that.'

'Indeed?'

'Apart from the vulgar hyperbole, which would have been enough for most educated people, there's no such thing as *Oeufs Américains à l'Orgueil*. Did you ever have it, by the way?'

'We did not.'

'You did believe it existed, though?'

'I didn't think about it.'

'But you didn't suspect the whole thing was a fraud and go down to prove it?'

'Certainly not,' Mr de Blame had said. 'I wanted a luxurious and quiet holiday and that is what they offered me.'

'Your letter of acceptance rather suggests that you might have had legal advice first. Why did you say, in effect, that you were going down on the strength of their representations?'

'Because I wanted them to know it. I had been had before.'

'When?'

'Every time I've been to an English hotel almost.'

'Then you did suspect something on this occasion. You must have, if you'd nearly always been had in the past.'

'I believe people till I find them out. Naturally I knew it was possible that the language meant nothing, because I'd seen that sort of thing before, but I hoped it was different this time. And I certainly wouldn't have gone if they'd replied that my assumption was incorrect. Now, tell me, Mr Trent, is there any chance that I shall lose the action?'

'*Any* chance? There's always a chance, of course, in any action. But, if your evidence is believed, you'll win.'

'And do you think I will be believed? I happen to be telling the truth, and my wife too, but naturally you don't know that for certain yet.'

'I wouldn't say that you were not capable of telling an untruth if it suited you, Mr de Blame,' Trent had said, 'but as far as this case goes, I should say that what you have told me is correct.'

'That's very kind of you, Mr Trent.'

'I'm not trying to be kind or unkind, Mr de Blame, just to let you know the position as I see it.'

After the conference Mr de Blame had expressed the hope to his solicitor that Trent was as able as he was irritating.

'He certainly is.'

'Then he'll go a very long way,' was Mr de Blame's reply.

After Trent had finished opening the case to Roger, he called his evidence. The case took Roger several days to try. Nothing that could possibly be worth mentioning had been left out from the plaintiff's case, while the defendants called as many guests as they could to say what a high standard was maintained at their hotel.

'It is not without significance', said Trent, in his closing speech, 'that one of these guests was eighty-seven, another was deaf and half-blind, while the only guest who could be described as *compos corporis et mentis* was a relation by marriage of Mrs Sweep.'

Eventually Roger gave judgement: 'It is, of course, well known', he said, 'that every vendor of goods and services is inclined to rate his commodities at too high a worth. But every reasonable man knows that these puffs must be discounted or completely ignored. They know, too, that hotel brochures are no exception to the rule. The picture of the lounge is often taken at such an angle that you might imagine that it was the length of a cricket pitch, whereas in fact two men with long arms could span it from wall to wall. An hotel proprietor is allowed to speak highly of his hotel without running the risk of an action for fraud or breach of contract, provided he does not speak of it in such a way that the ordinary reasonable man would say on learning the true facts – "This is plainly untrue."

'It is also right that I should say, in view of some of the plaintiff's complaints and the defendant's answers thereto, that no vendor of goods is bound to advertise any disadvantages in those goods. But, as Mr Justice Darling (as he then was) observed very many years ago, in a case where a clergyman had been induced, by a travelling bucket-shop proprietor, to buy some worthless shares – "although an itinerant vendor of fish need not cry 'stinking fish, stinking fish', yet, if he knows that his fish do stink, he is not entitled to cry 'fresh fish, fresh fish', nor is he any the more entitled to do this if he happens to know that his customer cannot smell."

'I am not saying,' continued Roger, 'that in this case Mr de Blame, the plaintiff, could not smell. I think he could. I think he suspected that Mr and Mrs Sweep might not be able to make good their representations. But, on the other hand, I am quite satisfied that he and his wife went to the Grand Hotel for a holiday and not for the purpose of experiencing an action in the Queen's Bench Division.

'Now, one of the first questions I have to decide is whether any, and if so what, meaning is to be attached to the expression *de luxe*. May any hotel, however shabby its appearance, however poor its food and accommodation, so describe itself? In my view, that must to some extent depend upon the price asked. In these days no one could expect an hotel, however described, to provide high-quality food, service, and accommodation for, say, five guineas a week, and the use of the word *de luxe* in connection with an hotel making such a charge would not really have any effect. But when an hotel describes itself as *de luxe* and charges forty-five guineas per week for two persons, I think the words do have some meaning, and that a person going to such an hotel is entitled to expect a reasonably high standard of comfort and cooking. No more than a reasonably high standard but no less. Now, the defendants in this case went a good deal further than merely describing their hotel as *de luxe*. They said that the cooking was superb. They also said, and whether in view of the evidence it was conscious or unconscious humour I do not pause to enquire, they also said that the service was "something that you have not experienced anywhere in this country since the war". The plaintiff said that he had experienced it only too often. In view of the other statements in the brochure the defendants' words clearly meant that the service was really good.

'Perhaps I might mention now that the defendants say that the brochure was printed when they were not short of staff and that unfortunately, when the plaintiff arrived, they were short. But, if a brochure becomes out of date, it must be suitably amended or withdrawn. If it becomes untrue, it is no excuse to say that it was once true. A person charged with falsely describing himself as a bachelor when, in fact, he was a divorced person, might just as well say that he was a bachelor when he was born.

'The plaintiff says, and I accept, that, when they arrived at the hotel, there was apparently no porter on duty. No one appeared to take in their luggage, an untidy young lady in the reception desk pushed the visitors' book towards them without a word, and Mr Sweep himself, who was sitting next to the girl, did not raise his eyes from the crossword puzzle which he was trying to solve. The girl banged her hand down on a bell. After five minutes the plaintiff ventured to mention that nothing had happened. Mr Sweep continued with his puzzle, and the girl gave a shout which might have been "Ernie". As no "Ernie" appeared, the plaintiff asked whether perhaps they could be shown to their room. The answer was that it was on the third floor and that the lift service was temporarily suspended. It is not surprising that by this time the plaintiff was comparing the statements made in the brochure somewhat unfavourably with his first impressions of the hotel. Before walking up to his room, the plaintiff spoke to Mr Sweep. He said, I suspect with more asperity in his voice than he indicated in the witness box: "Are you the manager?"

'Mr Sweep said that he was, and continued with his puzzle. The plaintiff asked what was going to be done about their luggage. Mr Sweep asked the young lady if she was looking after the plaintiff. She said that she was, and Mr Sweep returned to his puzzle. I am satisfied that it was in fact twenty minutes before the luggage was taken up to the plaintiff's room. This was done complainingly by a man with tousled hair in a vest and trousers.

'Not long afterwards the plaintiff and his wife came downstairs and went into the bar. There was a girl – munching something and painting her fingernails – behind it. The plaintiff ordered – to use his own language – "Two dry Martinis." The plaintiff complains that that is exactly what they got, that is, two glasses containing dry Vermouth and nothing else. Now the days have, I think, long passed when a judge should ask: "What is a dry Martini?" It would certainly be a feigned innocence on my part – an innocence which I do not feel that the short time I have been on the Bench would in any case entitle me to assume. A dry Martini consists of gin mixed with dry Vermouth, and stirred or shaken up with ice with a squeezed piece of lemon peel put into it. The Vermouth may be French or Italian, provided it is dry, but, whatever the nationality or brand of the Vermouth, the drink is known as a dry Martini. I do not have to enquire why a drink which, for example, may consist, so far as the alcohol is concerned, solely of an English brand of gin and a French brand of Vermouth, should be called a dry Martini, although the firm of Martini e Rossi has supplied no part of its contents. But, of course, the firm of Martini e Rossi do make a dry Vermouth, and it is true that there are places where, if you ask for a dry Martini, that is all you will get. No doubt it is an admirable drink, and I am not intending to cast the slightest aspersions on the Vermouth made by the firm in question. It is of the highest quality. But if a person wants gin and Vermouth, shaken up or stirred with ice, he is entitled to be dissatisfied if he is given instead some dry Vermouth rather warm. I think Mr Trent, on behalf of the plaintiff, is fully entitled to say that an establishment which can properly describe itself as *de luxe* and which charges what I may call *de luxe* prices should know what is meant by a dry Martini.

'It is not altogether surprising that by this time the plaintiff was becoming extremely angry, and I am careful to approach the rest of his evidence with caution, for it would have taken an exceptionally good dinner, beautifully served, to have pacified him. But I am bound to say that neither Mr nor Mrs Sweep did anything whatever to pacify their guests. It may be that, as their rooms were all full and booked up for some time, they did not mind. All they did, when complaint was made about the dry Martini, was to tell the girl to put in some gin. This she did with a toss of her head – or perhaps I should have said, to prevent any misunderstanding, tossing her head, she poured some gin into the plaintiff's glass and that of his wife. The plaintiff says the gin was also warm, and I believe him.

'The next complaint is about the dinner itself, both as to its component parts and as to the manner in which it was served. I once heard a caterer, who was being asked to quote for supplying refreshments to a small society, say disparagingly, when the secretary indicated that their requirements were much more modest than the caterer had suggested: "We call that giving them a cup of tea and throwing a bun at them." I must say that the evidence satisfies me that that was the sort of dinner this *hotel de luxe par excellence* supplied. I think, too, that when the plaintiff said: "A hot waitress steamed across the room hissing, 'thick, clear, or sardine,' " I was given a fair idea of what the plaintiff had to endure. Only on one point do I find against the plaintiff in this connection. He complains that cabbage was served and that it was a soggy mess. I quite agree with the plaintiff that that *might* be a ground for complaint. But, having regard to the fact that that is the normal way of dealing with that delicious vegetable, even in restaurants of acknowledged excellence, I cannot hold that against the defendants. I do not think that their cabbage, almost tasteless and ruined as it was, was any worse than that which is normally supplied, up and down the country, by cooks and chefs of every description. I regret to say that the same abominable treatment of cabbage takes place in many homes, too. That what was served to the plaintiff was a soggy mess, I accept, but that apparently is all the Englishman expects of cabbage, even in the most exclusive restaurants and clubs. At any rate that is what he gets, and will continue to get unless and until better taste prevails.

'For the rest, I can only say that the standard prevailing at the defendants' hotel was far below the standard which had been represented to the plaintiff as existing at the Grand, however much one discounts the exaggerated description of its delights. I am satisfied that the standard at the time of the plaintiff's visit was that of a very second-rate or third-rate hotel. I am afraid that persons in the position of the defendants, and other hotel proprietors too, take advantage of the unwillingness of the public to make a fuss, let alone make such a fuss as the plaintiff has made in this case. In my opinion he has performed a public service in calling the attention of hotel proprietors to their obligations to their customers. The plaintiff is accordingly entitled to receive damages and I shall now proceed to assess them.'

Roger went on to award the plaintiff one hundred and fifty pounds with costs on the High Court scale.

Mr de Blame thanked Trent and his junior cordially before leaving the Court.

'May I say', he said, 'that it was a *de luxe* performance *par excellence*.'

Trent thought for a moment, then: 'Thank you,' he said, 'I don't think I made many mistakes.'

'Roger, you were quite splendid,' said Anne, as they left the Court together. 'I couldn't have said it better myself.'

'What vegetables are we having for dinner?' asked Roger. 'Cabbage?'

CHAPTER FIVE

Three Speeches

Roger's Circuit followed the usual custom of giving the new High Court judge a dinner.

'Have you thought what you're going to say tonight?' said Anne, on the morning of the day when it was to take place.

'It all depends,' said Roger. 'I'm no good at this sort of thing. I think I shall rely upon the inspiration of the moment. I wish Henry were going to be there.'

'To tell you what to say, or to lead the applause?'

'Both,' said Roger.

In the end he found it easier than he had expected. His health was proposed by the senior member of the Circuit, a very old man of nearly ninety, who never missed occasions of this kind. After a few preliminary remarks, the old man went on: 'They make them younger now. Perhaps it's a good thing. Perhaps it isn't. They last longer, of course, so the country gets more for its money, which is an advantage – I suppose. Though so much is spent by the government today that I can't think that the extra amount involved in appointing judges who are nearer to their appointment with the Great Judge would be noticed. I'm from the old school and I must confess I prefer the older type of judge.

'Roger Thursby will not, I trust – in spite of the tendency which I am told he has, to accept words at their face value – a tendency which I trust he will sometimes repress when listening to evidence – in spite of that tendency he will not, I am sure, think that I am expressing any disapproval of his appointment. Indeed, no. If one is to have whipper-snappers as judges, I couldn't think of a worthier whipper-snapper. And in ten or twelve years, or in fifteen at any rate, he will probably be a very good judge. As soon as that happens, no doubt he will retire.

'But personally I don't think you've had enough experience at – how old are you? Forty-six? at forty-six. When I was a young man of forty-six I knew very little. I thought I knew a lot, of course. As, no doubt, does Roger Thursby. I hope he does, anyway, because if he doesn't, nobody else will.

'I think the right age for a judge to be appointed is fifty-five to sixty. At any time from then on you may be making arrangements to pack your bags and join the Heavenly Circuit. I think that's a good thing. It has a sobering effect. But at anything under fifty, you're old enough to have played yourself in and at the same time the end of the innings appears so far ahead that you don't have to worry about it. So the besetting sin of pride is allowed, if not free rein, at any rate too much, and there is probably no sin which sits more unfortunately underneath the scarlet and ermine. You cannot do justice to your fellow men if you are at any stage of a case being influenced by your own personal pride. As one gets older one understands more and one's pride recedes accordingly. I am not frightened of losing face any more, but at forty-six I certainly was.

'Well, enough of that, but don't think I've finished. Dear me no. My innings will soon be over, I shall soon be on my way back to the pavilion. But I can still see the ball, I can still make a stroke or two, and even take a wicket.'

The old man paused and sipped his port.

'That was for my health, not yours,' he said.

'Now, what can I say about our new young judge?' he went on. 'He wasn't born when I was called to the Bar. Nothing like it. I doubt very much if his parents were married. Don't misunderstand me – I doubt if they'd met each other by then. So Roger Thursby was very much an off chance when I was called. Well, I didn't get on as fast as he did. Everything, I think, was slower in those days. It took me ten years to earn seven hundred and fifty pounds in the year. Of course, it was worth more in those days, but I fancy most people would not consider two and a half times that sum a satisfactory income today after ten years' practice. But let me tell you that I was one of the successful ones. I say that in no sense of boasting. Nor do I mean that there were not men who did not do far better. Of course there were. But in my day for a junior of reasonably average ability to have reached the seven hundred and fifty pound mark after ten years was quite good going. And you must remember that, once you reach that figure, you are likely either to go on pretty quickly or to stay at it and then to recede.

'I'm glad to say I went on. I took silk after twenty years. Our young friend here took it after, I believe, twelve, when he was about thirty-three. And thirteen years later, he's on the Bench. Well, that, I suppose, is the modern idea, but I don't agree with it at all. That isn't sour grapes. I should have hated to become a judge. That's not my type of life at all. Nothing – nothing could compensate me for losing the friendly atmosphere of the Bar. I should hate to sit up there all alone. No one to have a chat to, no one to sympathize when the old fool up there – it should be young fool now, I suppose – does something particularly stupid.

'And then again, there's another aspect of the matter. Everyone at the Bar is an advocate, and it must feel very strange having no case to press. I have known judges, I'm afraid, who remained advocates when they went on the Bench, who swiftly took sides with one litigant or the other and who ran the case as hard as they could for the side they favoured. Such men should never have become judges. They seldom give an appearance of justice and often actually do injustice. From what I hear of our young friend I don't think he suffers from that fault – I should have preferred to have been able to call it disqualification.

'Although for the purpose of proposing his health I have made the most careful enquiries into his virtues and vices, I've been unable to find any. Any vices, I mean. Except the one to which I referred earlier in my speech – of taking people too literally. Even that has an advantage. It should make counsel appearing before him choose their language carefully. And anything which may raise the standard of English at the Bar is an advantage. I regret to say that at the moment, when occasionally I go into Court, I am appalled at some of the things I hear. If counsel had addressed the Court in my young days as some do now, he would have received as serious a rebuff from some judges, as if today he appeared improperly dressed. Is it too late – I fear it is, but I shall make the plea just the same – is it too late to put in a plea for better language and better diction? I am in no way criticizing the American language for, although originally English, admittedly it is today a separate language; but must we use it in our Courts? I do hope that the younger men present today will take some notice of what I am saying. Go to the picture houses or the cinemas or whatever you call them, by all means, enjoy yourselves as you will, but do not, I pray, use the language you hear there in the course of your professional duties, any more than you use the language of the public house in your own home.

'Well, I have gone on too long – tonight, I mean – I hope that my innings as a whole will continue a little yet – if only to see whether Mr Justice Thursby becomes Lord Justice Thursby – God help us – before he is fifty – and I have said little in favour of our guest of honour. There is still time for a word or two. I am quite sure that he would not have been appointed at his early age if he did not possess in a high degree those qualities which are required in one of Her Majesty's judges, modesty, integrity, knowledge of the law, understanding of human nature – phew! what a paragon he must be – and the list isn't finished yet – next comes patience and, finally, an ability to keep quiet. And, as an example to him, that is what I shall now do. I give you the toast of Mr Justice Thursby, may he live long and happily, may he judge well and humbly.'

And the old man sat down. When he had said that his criticisms were not made as a result of sour grapes, the older men in his audience knew that that was indeed true. The old man had in his earlier days been offered a High Court Judgeship more than once, had even been pressed to take it, but, for the reasons he gave during his speech, he had always refused.

When the clapping had died down, Roger was called on to respond. After the normal beginning he went on: 'Kendall Grimes was my master in the law. I learned a lot from him. But it took a year. And he was a member of the Bar. I feel that today, in little more than five minutes, I have learned from someone who has never been a judge

– though we all know that he could have been one if he had wished – I have learned more about judges in those few minutes than in a whole year I learned about advocacy. Then, of course, I am older. I am not twenty-one any longer. I am – God and the proposer forgive me – forty-six. Listening to the proposer I couldn't help wishing that I could have had in my pocket some gadget on the lines of H G Wells' time machine, which would have enabled me to add a year or two to my age before I had to reply. I could then have begun by saying: "I was forty-six when you began, but now I am fifty-five." Indeed, we have all heard speeches – though certainly not tonight – where one might have said that with feeling, if not with truth.

'Most people that I know – of either sex – want to take a few years off their ages, not to add to them. But, to tell you the truth – and in a gathering such as this I see no objection to telling the truth – it is not as if we were in Court – to tell you the truth, I am very happy with my years – all forty-six of them, and my only regret is that they should seem too few to the proposer. If only my parents had known his views on the subject, I'm sure they would have done what they could to have speeded things up a bit. But I'm afraid their best efforts would not have added more than a couple of years, for, with the best will in the world, when one is in New Zealand and the other in this country – in those days at any rate – nothing more than fine words could have been achieved. And, as we know, fine words cannot even butter parsnips.

'But to return to the situation as it is, not as it might have been – not only am I entirely happy with my years, but, I confess, they seem to add to their number with extraordinary rapidity, so that – even without one of Mr Wells' gadgets – I seem to be travelling along the road of time pretty fast. But I try to keep on my proper side, to maintain a good lookout, to pay full consideration to others using the road, and to stop whenever I come to a halt sign. In the words of one of our most distinguished judges – halt to me means halt.

'But I can't pretend I've always done that. There were times in my earlier days, when, though I may have paused momentarily at the red light, I went across before it changed to green. The proposer is quite right. The experience of age does teach one to be – to be careful. There are things I would do differently today if I had my time over again.

'But I can't say that I should like the opportunity, even if I were promised that I should start my career at twenty-one with the knowledge which I now have. I don't think I could bear to see the horror on the face of the judge when the white-wigged, white-faced little boy proceeded to deliver him a lecture – and a good one too – I've read *Central Property* and Hightrees – on the one-time doctrine of consideration. After all, I have seen my good friend Tony Trent at work – indeed I've felt him at it too. It's a joy to hear him – always has been – but one, I think, is enough. No, I don't want to go back and, of course, I can't – and I am quite happy to go forward, and I must.

'How far I go forward – in the sense referred to by the proposer of this toast – is quite another matter, and I can only hope that, if the worst should happen – and personally as an optimist I see no reason why it should – I hope that I shall bear the situation with the same fortitude as that with which the proposer of this toast has borne my unexpected advancement to the Bench. I leave you to judge what I mean by the worst.

'Now, the proposer has said that he hopes I think I know a lot. Well, I don't know a lot, but nevertheless I think that by now there must be a legal presumption that

I do. I was twenty-one when I was told that I had a lot to learn. That was twenty-five years ago. Presumably, on the principle of *id certum est quod certum reddi potest*, or, if you prefer it, *omnia rite ac sollenniter*, etc., a principle, I may say, which stood me in good stead on my first day at the Bar, when I was left before the Official Referee with a brief I hadn't looked at – though it wouldn't have made the slightest difference at that stage if I'd read it through ten times – on one or other of those principles I must now be presumed in law to have learned a lot. After all, twenty-five years is a reasonable time, and am I not right in thinking that in law everything which can be done can be done in a reasonable time? At any rate, if any member of the Circuit thinks that there is a fallacy somewhere, I will be delighted to hear him on the subject in a suitable place after the adjournment.

'In case, however, I get no further opportunity of thanking you each individually, I do want now to thank you all, and particularly the proposer of this toast, for your hospitality, kindness, and good wishes. I have been extremely lucky and my good fortune has pursued me up till this very moment – for how many judges have had the good fortune to have been given at my early stage on the Bench the benefit of such wisdom? I only hope that my luck may continue and that I shall have the good sense and ability to take advantage of what I have heard tonight.

'Could there be a finer motto for the coat of arms of a judge than *Sapientia ac humilitate*? I said finer, not more modest, for most people choose their coat of arms, though seldom their epitaph. That does happen, though, and I should have expected Tony Trent to have jotted the words down on his cuff, but for the fact that, as soon as I made the suggestion, I saw the words leap into the store-house of his prodigious memory – where they will remain until he is giving instructions to his executors.

'Some time ago I suggested to a member of the Court of Appeal as a motto – *per incuriam nihil*, and now I come to think of it the two might stand together: *Sapientia ac humilitate: nil per incuriam*. The only objection is, that I doubt if the motto, as a whole, would be true of any judge. When Tony Trent becomes a judge, I should be prepared to concede the first and last, but even he wouldn't claim the middle word. As for myself, I cannot at the moment claim the right to any of them, but I shall at least have those words as targets to aim at and, if I keep aiming in the right direction, there is always a chance that I might hit something.

'I cannot hope that the members of this Circuit will always approve my judgements – for that would mean that none of them would ever appear before me – but I do hope that you will all consider that, even if my weapons are of poor quality, I shall use them to the best of my ability, and that, even if I have neither modesty, integrity, nor most of the other qualities which the proposer detailed as being essential to my position – and it is rather hard that he should single out almost every quality in which I failed my forty-six plus – I hope you will consider that he and I have this one quality in common – that we know when to sit down. Thank you all very, very much.'

By the custom of the Circuit there were only three speeches on these occasions. The third was normally put in the hands of an accomplished wit, who was supposed to propose the health of the Circuit, and this toast was not replied to. The committee thought it would be amusing to employ Anthony Trent, who readily obliged: 'This is becoming a habit,' he began. 'When the judge first sat, I welcomed him with a few well-chosen words, and now –

although the honour of proposing his health has been denied me – I am at least the only other speaker. When I become a judge – or should I say if – I'm not sure what etiquette demands – but no one – not even the judge himself – would ever accuse me of false modesty – I have always said what I really thought of myself – when or if I become a judge, I hope that I shall discharge my duties on occasions such as this, at least as well as my good friend Roger Thursby.

'No one can say that I have not been one to profit by my own mistakes – for I *have* made them in the past, yes, indeed – but, if I have profited by my own, I have profited even more by the mistakes made by other people. So now, when – if and when – my turn comes, I shall know what to say and what not to say, and I hasten to add there was very little indeed that fell from the judge that was not entitled to a very high mark. His speech, if I may say so, struck just the right note and, apart from the actual phraseology and construction here and there, could hardly have been better.

'Although my duty tonight is limited to proposing the health of ourselves – and I think I may take it as no coincidence that I was chosen for this purpose – I do not think I shall be liable to a fine for Circuit misconduct if I say in all sincerity – I wish I could add humility – what personal pleasure it has been to me to see the well-deserved success our new judge promises to have. I have already appeared before him several times, and I can assure him that such errors as he made were all of a kind which are only to be expected from a newly-appointed judge, even – if I may say so – from one of more mature years. I may add that his manner was friendly but judicial, his language entirely adequate (one cannot expect every judge to have the same command of words as the late

Lord Hewart), and, I am glad to assure you, infrequent. In all, he is likely to maintain the high traditions of the English Bench and to add to the renown of this Circuit, whose health it gives me the greatest pleasure to propose.'

CHAPTER SIX

Mr Saul-Bibury

Anne was waiting up for Roger when he got home, and he told her all about the dinner.

'Did you go down well?' she asked.

'Oh, all right,' said Roger. 'After all, if they give a chap a dinner, they've got to pretend to listen to him, and to applaud him when – it may be because – he sits down. At any rate, I didn't make a mistake I once heard made. After a particularly witty speech a very dull fellow got up and spoke at inordinate length. Halfway through he was incautious enough to say that he wished he could have spoken in the same cheerful and witty vein as the last speaker. "I'm with you there, sir," said a very bored and somewhat inebriated diner.'

'I'm sure you spoke well,' said Anne. 'I wish I could have heard you.'

'I wish you could have heard old Hitchcock. He really was magnificent. He ought to give a course of lectures to judges. Some of them could do with it.'

'You talk as though you were still at the Bar,' said Anne. 'Don't forget, you'd have to attend.'

Roger laughed.

'How right you are. I'll probably be as bad as any of them. The trouble is, no one will tell us. If Henry had still been at the Bar, he might have. But most judges have only their powers of self-observation to guide them. And some of those I've known must either have been pretty weak in that respect or have had very odd ideas of what a judge should be. Why, the very man who said "Justice must not only be done but it must manifestly be seen to be done" was a glaring example. Justice was, no doubt, often done in his Court, but it sometimes required more than a Bisley marksman's eye to observe it.'

'Well, I'll come and listen to you and paint you a picture afterwards.'

'Unvarnished?' said Roger.

'The truth, the whole truth and nothing but the truth.'

'You're a darling,' said Roger, and kissed her.

'I have to pinch myself sometimes,' he said after a few moments. 'It's odd to think that I'm really a judge. Most of the public think of us as awe-inspiring figures, completely removed from ordinary everyday affairs. It must feel very like contempt of Court to think of a judge indulging in the ordinary daily routine of life – to visualize the terrible red-robed figure getting into a bath – quite naked.'

'Darling,' said Anne, 'you won't take yourself too seriously, will you? I think that most people must realize that there is a human being under all that clutter.'

The next day had been fixed for a weekend visit to Henry and Sally.

Anne went down in the morning and looked very charming sitting next to Henry on the Bench. And Mr Saul-Bibury did not let Henry down. He was there. He was a prosperous-looking gentleman of middle age, always well dressed and always with no money but prodigious prospects. On this particular morning his name appeared six times in Henry's list. That accounted for the attendance of two young counsel, one a very pretty girl and one a young man rather like Roger had been. In addition there were three solicitors representing three of the creditors, and a creditor in person, a Mr Crewett, who had sold Mr Saul-Bibury some chickens for which he had not been paid.

It was the first time anyone had bilked Mr Crewett. He considered himself a shrewd judge of character, and when the prosperous-looking Mr Saul-Bibury drew up in a large car and placed an order with him, to be sent to a prosperous-sounding address, he readily accepted the excuse that Mr Saul-Bibury had accidentally left his cheque book behind. As a matter of fact it was quite true. He had left his cheque book behind. And it was by accident. Mr Saul-Bibury would have been very happy to have given a cheque to Mr Crewett. He often gave cheques to his creditors, but, as none of them were ever met, it made not the slightest difference to anyone.

As soon as Mr Saul-Bibury's name was called, Mr Crewett leaped to his feet and rushed into the witness box. He had already noticed that that was the place for litigants who were not represented.

'Your Honour,' he said, 'I don't know much about these things, but will you please read these documents before you begin?'

He handed to the clerk a bundle of letters and some legal papers.

'Very well,' said Henry. 'If no one minds, I'll look at them. But I'm afraid, Mr Crewett, that I have seen letters from Mr Saul-Bibury before, and they may not shock me as much as they might shock some people.'

'All I want is justice,' said Mr Crewett.

'It's sometimes very difficult for creditors to get what they call justice,' said Henry, 'but let me see the letters.'

The clerk handed the bundle to Henry, who could not resist reading it from beginning to end. It began with a letter from Mr Crewett to Mr Saul-Bibury.

> Hamlet Saul-Bibury Esq.
> Hermon Lodge
> Pendlebury.

Dear Sir,
 I have pleasure in enclosing my account for the goods I supplied you last month.
   Assuring you of my best attention,
     Yours faithfully,
> Samuel Crewett

Mr Saul-Bibury never considered it necessary to answer at that stage.

The next letter was still in courteous terms:

> With reference to the account I delivered to you last month for £35 9s. 3d. I should be greatly obliged if you would favour me with a remittance as I am completing my quarterly stocktaking at the end of next week.
> In the hope that I may still be of service to you, I am, etc.

Mr Saul-Bibury remained unmoved at that second stage also. The third letter ran:

> I am a little surprised to have had no settlement of the account I sent you two months ago in spite of my last letter, and I should be most grateful if you would effect an early settlement. Still assuring you of my best attention.

That letter was answered after about a fortnight.

> Dear Mr Crewett,
>   Thank you so much for your last letter. I have been looking everywhere for your account, but it must have been mislaid. I am so very sorry for the delay. Would you be kind enough to send me another account at once? I am going away for some weeks, and should like to settle it before I go.

That letter was postmarked some seven or eight days after it was dated, and Mr Crewett assumed that, when he sent his account by return of post, it must have missed Mr Saul-Bibury.

In fact it did not miss Mr Saul-Bibury, who put it with the previous letters and accounts, and a good many others, into the wastepaper basket or the fire, according to the time of year.

Two months later, Mr Crewett returned to the attack.

> If you are now back from your holidays, I shall be much obliged if you will settle the enclosed account, which is now long overdue.

The 'if you are now back' was a fatal mistake. Mr Crewett received the following reply:

> In the absence of Mr Saul-Bibury, I have opened your letter and know that Mr Saul-Bibury will be very distressed to learn on his return that your account is so long overdue. Please accept my assurance that the matter will be placed before Mr Saul-Bibury immediately on his return, when a cheque will no doubt be sent.

An illegible signature followed, which Mr Saul-Bibury very much enjoyed writing above the typewritten word 'secretary'.

Mr Crewett replied to the 'Secretary to Hamlet Saul-Bibury' saying:

> I shall be much obliged if you will let me know when you are expecting Mr Saul-Bibury to return.

After a week, Mr Saul-Bibury replied:

> I have written to Mr Saul-Bibury asking him to let me have the information you requested. I also suggested, I hope with your approval, that if he receives my letter he should send me a cheque to enable me to clear your account. I asked Mr Saul-Bibury to telegraph me if he received my letter, but I regret to say that so far no wire has been received. I am afraid that this means he must have missed my letter. In this case I shall write to him at the next address he sends me.

After a few more letters of this kind Mr Crewett's patience began to be exhausted:

> It is really too bad, he wrote. These goods were supplied almost a year ago and it is quite outrageous that there has been no settlement. Unless I receive a remittance within the course of the next fourteen days I shall issue a summons in the County Court.

Within the fourteen days a reply was received:

> I am sure you will be pleased to hear that I have this day heard from Mr Saul-Bibury that he will be returning here within the next two or three weeks, or

at the most a month, when your account will at once be placed before him for immediate settlement.

A month went by. Mr Crewett then wrote:

Unless I receive a remittance within seven days a summons will be issued.

Within the seven days came a letter from Mr Saul-Bibury:

Dear Mr Crewett,
I am so very sorry that settlement of your account has been delayed so long. If only I had received it before I went away it would have been paid long ago. Unfortunately my secretary has been taken suddenly ill and has had to leave me, and my accounts are, I am afraid, in complete disorder. Would you be good enough to send me a copy of your account, and I will send you a cheque?

The account was sent by return.
Three days went by. Then:

Dear Mr Crewett,
I duly received your account but as it gives no details and only says 'to account rendered', I should be grateful if you would let me have the details, as you will understand that, after this long time, I have completely forgotten the transaction.

The words 'after this long time' nearly choked Mr Crewett, but he sent a detailed bill by return of post, with a threat that, if it were not paid immediately, proceedings would follow.

The debt was now nearly two years old.
Within the stipulated time, Mr Saul-Bibury wrote:

Dear Mr Crewett,

I am so very sorry that payment of this account has been so long delayed, and I should like to thank you for your patience in the matter. Although I am not at all clear as to the three items of £11 3s. 7d., £4 6s. 9d. and £17 2s. 3d., and believe there may be some mistake about them, it would not be reasonable to query them at this stage and accordingly I have pleasure in enclosing my cheque for £35 9s. 3d.

Thanking you again for your forbearance,

Yours sincerely,

Hamlet Saul-Bibury

Enclosed was a cheque for thirty-five pounds nine shillings and threepence in words and £34 9s. 3d. in figures. It was dated a year ahead and unsigned. Mr Saul-Bibury had found by experience that errors of date and figures often passed unnoticed if the cheque was unsigned. The absence of signature usually struck the creditor with such force that, with a suitable oath, he put the cheque in an envelope and sent it back. When the bank pointed out the other errors it was as much the creditor's fault as that of Mr Saul-Bibury. Mr Crewett noticed at once the lack of signature and the errors in the figures, but he missed the mistake in the year. Mr Saul-Bibury apologized profusely for the errors and sent back a letter saying that the corrected and duly signed cheque was enclosed, although it was not.

Your letter did not enclose the cheque. I am issuing a summons,

wrote Mr Crewett.

Back came the cheque duly signed, with the amount in words and figures correct, but still dated a year ahead. Mr Crewett sent the cheque to his bank, with instructions to have it specially cleared. When they pointed out to him that a cheque which is dated a year ahead cannot be cleared at all until the year is over, his wrath overflowed and the spittle with which he licked the envelope sending his next letter to Mr Saul-Bibury was pretty well boiling. Mr Saul-Bibury was full of apologies and sent back a cheque for the correct amount in words and figures, with the right date and duly signed.

Mr Crewett had only had this in his possession for half an hour when a telegram followed:

Do not present cheque. Letter follows.
Saul-Bibury

Mr Crewett presented the cheque immediately and it was duly returned 'Orders not to pay'.

At the same time he received Mr Saul-Bibury's promised letter.

Dear Mr Crewett,
I am so sorry to have had to stop this cheque but you will remember that I wrote to you that I could not quite understand three of the items totalling £32 12s. 7d. I have now been further into the matter, and think you must have made a mistake and confused my account with someone else's. I enclose a cheque for the admitted balance in full and final settlement of your account.

Enclosed was a cheque for two pounds sixteen and eightpence which Mr Crewett indignantly returned under the mistaken impression that, if he accepted it, he would not have been able to recover the balance. In fact he lost nothing by returning the cheque, as even that would not have been met.

The bundle which Henry was reading also disclosed that the next step was a summons, which was duly served on Mr Saul-Bibury. To this Mr Saul-Bibury put in a long and elaborate defence which was worthy of any lawyer, and which compelled Mr Crewett to go to a local solicitor.

Now, Mr Crewett lived about a hundred and fifty miles from Mr Saul-Bibury, and he was able to issue the summons in his, Mr Crewett's, local Court. Mr Saul-Bibury promptly asked for a transfer to the Court of his own district on the ground that he would be unable to travel a hundred and fifty miles to make good his defence. With some hesitation the judge at Mr Crewett's local Court transferred the case to Pendlebury County Court and Mr Crewett had to make the long journey in order to prove his case. He had expected a long, blustering defence to be put up by Mr Saul-Bibury, and he was all ready for it. He brought up all his books, and his wife, who had been present when the original order was given, and he waited grimly for his case to be called on. When it was called, Mr Saul-Bibury was not present and Mr Crewett duly obtained judgement for thirty-five pounds nine and threepence.

But it is one thing to obtain judgement for thirty-five pounds nine and threepence – another thing to obtain the money. A bailiff was sent to levy execution on the goods and chattels of Mr Saul-Bibury at Hermon Lodge. Hermon Lodge was a small but comfortably furnished cottage. It was completely furnished on the hire-purchase system, except for the television set and the carpets, which belonged to Mrs Saul-Bibury. There was a large car in the garage, but this belonged to Mr Saul-Bibury's brother-in-law (who was an invalid and unable to drive) and, to make assurance doubly sure, was also being acquired on the hire-purchase system.

When the failure of this method of execution was reported to Mr Crewett, he duly issued a judgement summons and, in spite of the expense involved, he made the journey to Pendlebury County Court. He was going to have his money out of Mr Saul-Bibury, even if it cost him twice as much to get it.

Now, Mr Saul-Bibury knew as much about judgement summonses as most judges, and much more than some of them. He, indeed, could have explained what a '271' was, and he knew when it was safe to ignore a summons and when he must appear in Court. This was one of the occasions when it was necessary for him to appear. He could have obtained a doctor's illegible certificate but only to say that he was unfit for work due to 'Coryza', which looks impressive on a certificate, legible or illegible, but, to anyone who knows, means a cold. But he had used that method of delay sufficiently often with Judge Blagrove. Also it meant staying at home in case a bailiff called to see how he was, and, as he had several pleasurable appointments to keep in town, he decided that he must appear.

Henry finished reading the bundle which Mr Crewett had handed in. 'Very well,' he said, 'let the debtor be sworn.'

Mr Saul-Bibury stepped blandly and smilingly into the witness box, took the oath, and turned expectantly towards the advocates' row, rather like a good hotel manager welcoming guests to an expensive hotel.

'Yes, Mr Found?' said Henry. 'Would you like to open the innings? I'll hear Mr Crewett later.'

Mr Found, the chief local solicitor, rose ponderously. 'If your Honour pleases,' he said. Then he turned to the debtor.

'Well, Mr Saul-Bibury,' he said. 'Have you any offer to make?'

'To your client only or to everyone?' said Mr Saul-Bibury in reply.

'To my client at the moment,' said Mr Found.

Mr Saul-Bibury appeared to be deep in thought for a moment. Then he turned towards the Judge.

'I want to be fair to everyone, your Honour,' he said. 'At the moment I'm afraid there's only a very limited amount at my disposal. If all these summonses could be held over for three months I have every hope that they will be paid in full.'

'That's what you said three months ago,' said Henry.

'And three months before that,' put in Mr Bridle, another of the solicitors concerned.

'That's very true,' said Mr Saul-Bibury solemnly. 'No one is more sorry than I am that I have had to disappoint you all. Particularly your client, Mr Found, who, I freely admit, has been rather badly treated. Perhaps, your Honour, I could make a small offer to Mr Found's client and then the other cases can be adjourned?'

'How much is the offer?'

'Well, I'm afraid it can only be described as a token offer – just an earnest of good faith, your Honour.'

'Good faith!' spluttered Mr Crewett.

'How much?' said Mr Found.

'Ten shillings a month,' replied Mr Saul-Bibury.

'At that rate,' said Henry, 'it will take five years to settle this one debt, apart from the others.'

'It does seem a long time put like that,' conceded Mr Saul-Bibury. 'I wish I could make it more.'

'What are you living on?' demanded Mr Found.

'My friends and relations,' said Mr Saul-Bibury, smiling. 'I'm very lucky.'

'Have you no income at all?' said Mr Found.

'At the moment, no,' said Mr Saul-Bibury.

'Why don't you get a decent job? There are plenty going,' said Mr Found.

'What, at ten pounds a week?' said Mr Saul-Bibury. 'How could I pay my creditors if I did? If I took a full-time job I should be unable to follow up some propositions which have been put to me and which I have no doubt whatever will in due course enable me to pay everyone.'

'Yes, Mr Found,' said Henry, 'any further questions? No? Who's in next? Miss Paterson? Very well, then.' The pretty girl got up.

'Mr Saul-Bibury, you say you've no money, but isn't it true that you regularly dine at expensive restaurants in London?'

'Regularly?' queried Mr Saul-Bibury. 'No, I wouldn't say regularly.'

'Well, sometimes then?'

'Oh, yes, indeed. Last week perhaps your client saw me.'

'And how were you able to do that out of no income?'

'I wasn't paying, Miss Paterson.'

'Do you never pay?'

'Only when I have the money.'

'And when did you last have the money?'

Mr Saul-Bibury shook his head sadly. 'When indeed?' he said. 'I shall have a lot of hospitality to repay as well as my debts.'

'Mr Saul-Bibury,' said Miss Paterson, 'isn't it correct that you go about in a large car, eat well, drink well, clothe yourself well, and live in comfort and yet pay your creditors nothing?'

'It sounds bad put like that, I agree,' said Mr Saul-Bibury.

'How would you put it?' said Henry.

'It's not for me to appraise myself, is it, your Honour, with respect?'

'You don't seem to mind about your creditors at all,' said Henry.

'Oh, but I do, your Honour. If I didn't mind I would just go bankrupt.'

'How much have you paid your creditors in the last three years?' said Henry.

'In the last three years?' repeated Mr Saul-Bibury. 'They've been lean years, I'm afraid. Let's hope the next three will be fat and everyone will be happy.'

'Have you any offer to make to my client?' asked Miss Paterson.

'Well,' said Mr Saul-Bibury, 'if no one wants the ten shillings a month, your client can have it.'

'Where will you get that from?'

'Indeed,' said Mr Saul-Bibury, 'where shall I get it from? I shall have to reduce my smoking, I suppose.'

'Then you can afford to smoke?'

'Alas, no.'

'But you do smoke?'

'Alas, yes.'

'And drink?'

'Alas, yes.'

'Where do you get the money to do it from?'

'My friends and relations.'

'Then why can't you borrow the money from them to pay some of your creditors?'

'Oh, I don't get it in cash.'

'Then how could you pay ten shillings a month?'

'I'm not really sure that I could.'

'But you just said that you'd have to smoke less.'

'To tell you the truth, at the time I said that I was thinking of the days when I'd money of my own.'

'Then you can't offer even ten shillings a month?'

'No, I suppose I can't. But, as was pointed out, it would hardly be worth having anyway.'

'Now, Mr Crewett,' said Henry, 'would you like to ask this debtor any questions?'

'Yes, your Honour,' said Mr Crewett, 'I should.'

'Certainly,' said Henry.

Mr Crewett then started to put to Mr Saul-Bibury the correspondence leading up to the judgement, but he was soon interrupted by the judge.

'I'm afraid', said Henry, 'that none of this has anything to do with it. All I'm concerned with is whether the debtor could have paid the debt since judgement was obtained, not with how he put you off before then.'

'But it's fraud,' said Mr Crewett.

'If you think so,' said Henry, 'it is always open to you to go to the police. I'm not concerned with that.'

'Well, it isn't justice,' said Mr Crewett. 'I've come a hundred and fifty miles over this and it looks as though I might just as well have stayed at home.'

'I'm afraid', said Henry, 'that is perfectly true. Unless you really can show that a debtor has means, judgement summonses are a waste of time. I'm afraid Mr Saul-Bibury is a good example of that.'

'Everyone will be paid, your Honour,' said Mr Saul-Bibury, 'if they'll exercise a little patience. I had an appointment today, as a matter of fact, to discuss a most promising proposition but, unfortunately, I had to put it off in order to come here.'

'Patience!' exclaimed Mr Crewett. 'What have I been exercising for the last two and a half years?'

'I'm sorry about your case,' said Mr Saul-Bibury. 'I really am. The chickens were excellent, really excellent. I think I have treated you rather badly, too. But it wouldn't be right to give you a preference over my other creditors. *Pari passu* is, I think, the right expression. Share and share alike.'

'But what is there to share?' asked Henry.

'Ah,' said Mr Saul-Bibury. 'If your Honour will adjourn these summonses for three months, I may have a surprise for you all. Nothing would give me greater pleasure.'

And, as he said this, Mr Saul-Bibury beamed all round the court.

CHAPTER SEVEN

The Weekend

'Surely something can be done about a man like that,' said Anne, while she and Henry were having lunch.

'Not really,' said Henry. 'You saw six people trying without success.'

'But it's ridiculous,' said Anne.

'So it is in a way,' said Henry, 'but it's not as simple as you think. If any creditor could prove that Mr Saul-Bibury had obtained credit from him by fraud he could, of course, be prosecuted. Presumably they can't prove fraud or he'd have been prosecuted long ago.'

'Yes, but can't you make him pay? That's what they were asking you to do.'

'Yes, they were asking me to send him to prison unless he paid. Of course, in the old days, before Dickens' time, he could have been put into a debtors' prison until he paid. You wouldn't want to go back to those days, would you?'

'No, of course not, but there ought to be some way of making him pay,' said Anne.

'Well, if he hasn't any property of his own and you can't prove that he's had the means to pay the debt since judgement was obtained, there's nothing you can do except make him bankrupt. And that doesn't do much good.'

'Well, there's something wrong with the law, then.'

'I'm not so sure of that,' said Henry. 'You see, you're not bound to give a person credit. None of these creditors need have trusted the gentleman. Having chosen to do so they must accept the consequences. As I've said, if they could show that he'd cheated them into giving him credit they could prosecute him.'

'Well, I still say it's all wrong,' said Anne.

'A woman,' said Henry, 'is never convinced against her will. So there's not much more I can say, except that I hope you found him entertaining. He exudes goodwill, doesn't he? If that could be cashed, everyone would have been paid long ago. Tell me something quite different. You've seen Roger and me in Court now. How do we compare?'

'You talk more than he does,' said Anne.

'Good,' said Henry. 'Tell him to keep it up. The silent judges are the best.'

'Then why don't you talk less?'

'Well, it's more difficult to keep quiet in the County Court. It's what's known as an Inferior Court, as a solicitor I met at a cocktail party reminded me once. He said, rather pompously, that he thought that was unfair, as the County Court did important work. I couldn't resist saying that it was less unfair than calling solicitors members of the inferior profession. "They do important work, too," I said, "and some of them are knighted." He moved away after that. But it's quite true, really. The County Courts are much nearer to the people. Quite often litigants appear in person. Practically all judgement debtors do, for example. Well, I have to explain things to them, and I can't do that without talking, can I? Anyway, that's my story. The truth probably is that I do talk too much. But don't let Roger follow my bad example.'

After lunch they went into Court again. At 4.15p.m. Henry finished his list and he and Anne went back to his house until the time came to meet Roger's train. He arrived punctually and over dinner he told them the story of Plummer and Toni.

'I can't help liking the chap,' he said, 'I always did. But I'm terrified of what he'll do next.'

'Practical jokers are a menace,' said Henry. 'He ought to be locked up.'

'I know,' said Roger, 'but I bet you wouldn't have done any differently. However, let's hope he leaves me alone now, and turns his attention to a Cabinet Minister or something. No, I know,' he added, 'what about a County Court judge? I can tell him of one.'

'Too small fry,' said Henry, 'though I can't say I'd object if he brought a couple of his girl friends along. The one he allotted to you sounds ravishing.'

'I think she's probably a very decent girl,' said Roger. 'I'd really like to help her.'

'Help who?' said Henry.

'Her,' said Roger.

'Yes, I heard you,' said Henry. 'I was only wondering in my innocent little way if you'd be so keen on the Galahad touch if she looked like an unmade bed.'

'I think I can answer that,' said Sally.

'Well, of course I shouldn't,' said Roger, 'but what's that got to do with it? If she looked like that, she wouldn't need any help. Anne agrees with me, don't you?'

'Of course,' said Anne. 'I'd love to meet her.'

'Would you really?' said Roger, a little surprised at the warmth with which Anne had spoken, and pleased, too.

'But I couldn't ever be left alone with her again,' he added.

'Don't you trust yourself?' said Sally.

'Or don't you trust her?' said Henry.

'You know perfectly well what I mean,' said Roger. 'It's what you were talking about the day after I was appointed.'

'You mean', said Henry, 'that, if you were left alone with her, you might be manifestly seen to be bad?'

'Don't be ridiculous,' said Roger.

'Don't tease him,' said Anne. 'I expect he's had a much harder day than you have. You've just been enjoying yourself hearing debtors cheat their creditors.'

'Chambers want to give me a dinner,' said Roger. 'You'll come, won't you?'

'I'll come if I can,' said Henry. 'We might go to the Soft Shoe Club afterwards. Then I'd be able to meet Toni. Perhaps, even, I'd be allowed by Sally to help her sister.'

CHAPTER EIGHT

Libel on Ice

When Roger sat down in Court on the following Monday he looked anxiously to see if Plummer was in the audience, and was pleased to find that he was not. The case he had to try was unusual. It was a claim for damages for libel and the libel was said to be contained in an ice. Not on a piece of paper concealed in an ice cream or anything of that kind. The plaintiff complained that he was libelled by the ice itself.

The plaintiff was a local councillor, who had held various positions of importance in the borough where he lived, and the occasion of the alleged libel was a dinner which had been arranged in his honour. It was a very well organized dinner and, until the ice, the food was really superb. The caterers and the committee responsible for the dinner had both apparently set out to provide a dinner worthy of the guest of honour.

It began with smoked salmon of the finest quality; there were no little bits of dry, salty flesh with bones at the ready; a large generous portion, carefully cut, was served to each guest. It was followed by turtle soup, *sole Véronique*, and veal done in a specially delicious way. It was no wonder that, when the ice was served, the guests were ready for something quite out of the ordinary and that nearly everyone took a large mouthful and waited for it to melt happily in the mouth. There was another reason why they might expect something special. Up to the ice all the dishes had been simply described in French, but the ice was printed in slightly larger letters and was called *Bombe à la Marcus Jones* and it need hardly be said that Marcus Jones was the guest of honour. As the guests began to eat the ice the band struck up 'For he's a jolly good fellow', and all was set fair for the end of a perfect meal, apart from the coffee and liqueurs which were to follow.

The diners had been expecting something very special in the ice. They got it. It was a *pièce de résistance* with a vengeance. Whether it contained the flavour of cascara, bitter aloes, rancid butter, and senna pods, or a combination of one or more of these elements, was not quite certain at the time, but what was quite certain was that each guest after a momentary pause – as when the barber pours boiling water over the head of his customer and, for a split second, the victim thinks it is cold – gave a gasp which almost drowned the orchestra. Some of them swallowed it because it had gone too far, others because they were made of sterner stuff than the majority, who without hesitation redeposited what they could on their plates. Several rushed out of the room at once, and most of those who had swallowed it ran out shortly afterwards. It need hardly be said that the dinner was ruined and even the Chairman, who was renowned for his witty speeches, did not dare say anything which might make people laugh. Those of his audience who had remained were in no condition to laugh.

Mr Marcus Jones consulted his solicitor the next day. The caterers expressed the greatest regret and reduced their charges by half. They were entirely at a loss to explain how it had happened. The ice had been made of the finest ingredients and must have been tampered with. Someone must have gone to each portion and swiftly inserted the noxious substance with a syringe. But who and why? Marcus Jones' solicitor employed detectives to find out. And eventually they found a waiter who admitted that he had been paid by the defendant to do the deed. The defendant was a member of the Committee, and there was no doubt that in the past he and Marcus Jones had been on very bad terms.

Accordingly a libel action was brought by Mr Jones against the man in question, a Mr Tester.

Mr Jones alleged in his statement of claim, among other things: 'That by procuring the ice to be so named and at the same time to be so excruciatingly unpleasant the defendant meant and was understood to mean that the plaintiff was a very nasty man, that he made people sick and was nauseating to all his friends and acquaintances, that he was not fit to associate with his fellow citizens and that he ought to be ostracized by any reasonably minded civilized community.'

The defendant, though a wealthy man, conducted his own defence. In his written defence he agreed that the serving of the ice did mean that the plaintiff was all the things the plaintiff complained of, but, he said, they were true.

The plaintiff, he said, was a nauseating hypocrite, and the ice was but a poor relation of his.

Up till this point in his defence it looked as though the only question was whether the defendant could prove what was alleged against the plaintiff's character, and that the plot was admitted. But the defence ended by completely denying that the defendant had anything to do with the interference with the ice and went on to say that the plaintiff had, in fact, engineered it himself and persuaded the waiter to lie about the matter in order that he, the plaintiff, might bring this action.

It was not surprising, then, that, as soon as the case was reported in the newspapers, Roger's Court was crowded. The first part of the hearing soon developed into a slanging match between Mr Marcus Jones and Mr Tester. Two things swiftly emerged; that these gentlemen had long been enemies, and that neither of them was a particularly scrupulous person. For example, when Mr Tester put to Mr Jones that a close relation of his had had shares in a company to which the local authority had given a large contract, Mr Jones sought to parry the question by referring to similar conduct on the part of Mr Tester. At that stage Roger intervened and pointed out to Mr Jones that he must answer the questions properly.

After a day's cross-examination of the plaintiff by the defendant, it became pretty obvious to most people that, whatever might be uncertain in the case, it was quite certain that neither the plaintiff nor the defendant was fit to hold public office. It was odd, thought Roger, that reasoning beings should live like animals and indulge quite unnecessarily in a death struggle. Their hatred of each other made them completely unmindful of the consequence to themselves.

On the second day the plaintiff's counsel called the waiter. After he had given his name and address he was asked to give his account of the dinner and of anything he knew about the ice. At that stage Roger had to ask for a question to be repeated. He had just noticed that Plummer and Toni had come into Court. As Plummer was perfectly capable of preparing the ice-trick himself, Roger wondered, with a little apprehension, whether he had anything in store for the Court that day. Roger also noticed that Toni was looking particularly attractive. Two answers had to be repeated to him. In rebuking himself for his misbehaviour, Roger had the consoling thought that he was at any rate human. Much better than those strange creatures he had sometimes read about in fiction. But Toni really was lovely.

'Would you mind repeating the question, Mr Creamer?' Mr Creamer obliged:

MR CREAMER: And now tell his Lordship anything you know about the ice.

WAITER: About the ice?

MR CREAMER: Yes.

WAITER: It was served after the veal.

MR CREAMER: Yes, we all know that. What happened before it was served?

WAITER: They had the veal.

MR CREAMER: Mr Turner, did you have any conversation with the defendant, Mr Tester, before the dinner began?

WAITER: Any conversation?

MR CREAMER: Yes.

WAITER: About what?

MR CREAMER: About anything.

WAITER (*after a pause*): Well – I did – yes.

MR CREAMER: Where?

WAITER: In the street.

MR CREAMER: When?

WAITER: About a week before the dinner.

MR CREAMER: What was the conversation?

WAITER: Do I have to say?

ROGER: Do you mean that you are frightened of incriminating yourself?

WAITER: Of what, my Lord?

ROGER: Of getting into trouble. You don't want to answer in case it gets you into trouble, is that it?

WAITER: No, my Lord.

ROGER: Do you mean yes?

WAITER: No, my Lord.

ROGER: You mean you do want to answer?

WAITER: No, my Lord.

ROGER: Then you mean 'no'.

WAITER: Yes, my Lord.

ROGER: Well, Mr Creamer, what about it? The defendant is not represented, so I'd better hear what you say first. Is the witness bound to answer?

MR CREAMER: Why not, my Lord? It may be that at a later stage he will be privileged from answering. But how can it incriminate him merely to have to answer whether he was asked to do something by the defendant?

ROGER (*after a pause*): Very well, Mr Creamer, you may ask him if the defendant asked him to do anything, but I don't think he can be asked, if he objects, whether he agreed to do what he was asked – still less whether he did it.

MR CREAMER: If your Lordship pleases. Now, Mr Turner, did the defendant ask you to do anything?

WAITER: Yes. He asked me if I'd get an opportunity of squirting something into the ice.

ROGER: I gather you'd rather not answer any more questions on this subject?

WAITER: No, my Lord.

ROGER: You mean you don't want to answer further questions?

WAITER: Yes, my Lord.

ROGER: You mean – no you don't?

WAITER: Yes, my Lord.

ROGER: Very well, Mr Creamer, have you anything else you want to ask this witness?

MR CREAMER: Yes, my Lord, but your Lordship won't let me ask it.

So Mr Creamer sat down and Roger asked the defendant if he would like to cross-examine the waiter. He said that he would, and began at once:

DEFENDANT: Mr Turner, you're a man of bad character, aren't you?

WAITER: Do I have to answer that?

ROGER: Yes, I'm afraid so.

WAITER: Well, I know worse.

DEFENDANT: I dare say you do – the plaintiff, for example.

ROGER: Mr Tester, you mustn't make remarks like that. It's most improper. Ask the witness questions and don't comment on his answers, please.

DEFENDANT: I'm sorry, my Lord. Very well, Mr Turner, you know worse men than yourself. Where did you meet them – in prison?

WAITER: Do I have to answer that?

ROGER: Yes. You must understand, Mr Turner, that, while a witness is not bound to incriminate himself, he is bound to answer about any past crimes for which he has paid the penalty. Answering such questions does not incriminate you. You couldn't be charged with those offences again.

WAITER: I could get the sack.

ROGER: I'm afraid that doesn't excuse you from answering.

WAITER: I didn't want to come here to give evidence.

ROGER: I'm afraid I can't help that. You must answer the question. Will you repeat it, Mr Tester.

DEFENDANT: Have you been to prison?

WAITER: Yes.

DEFENDANT: How many times?

WAITER: Three – no, four.

DEFENDANT: Don't hurry yourself. Sure it's only four?

WAITER: Yes, quite. I went there – I ought to know.

DEFENDANT: What was the longest stretch?

WAITER: Three years.

DEFENDANT: What for?

WAITER: They called it fraud.

DEFENDANT: And what would you have called it? Business?

WAITER: Have I got to answer that?

ROGER: No, I don't think so. Any other questions, Mr Tester?

DEFENDANT: Yes, my Lord. Now, Mr Turner, you've just said that I asked you to spoil the ice. Didn't you tell me that Mr Jones himself asked you to do it?

WAITER: Have I got to answer that?

ROGER: Yes.

WAITER: Well – yes, I did.

DEFENDANT: Well, that was true, wasn't it – it was really he who asked you, not I? And he's paid you to say the opposite?

WAITER: Have I got to answer that?

ROGER: I'm not sure. I should like your help, Mr Creamer. The witness has sworn that the defendant asked him to interfere with the ice. He is now in effect asked whether that piece of evidence is not perjury. Of course if his answer were 'no' it would not amount to any admission, but if his answer were 'yes' he could surely be prosecuted, could he not?

MR CREAMER: Witnesses are often asked whether their evidence is not perjured.

ROGER: Of course they are, and normally they answer indignantly that it isn't. But surely, if a witness is asked if he has not told on oath a deliberate lie on a material matter, and the judge is satisfied that his objection to answering the question is a genuine one, the objection should be allowed?

MR CREAMER: Well, my Lord, I'm in your Lordship's hands.

ROGER: Very well, Mr Turner, tell me this. Are you frightened of answering the question Mr Tester asked you because you might be prosecuted for perjury if you answered it?

WAITER: Yes, my Lord. I've had enough trouble as it is.

ROGER: Very well, then, you need not answer the question, but, in view of your evidence, would the plaintiff and the defendant like to consider composing their differences? After all, whatever is the truth of this matter, no one can rely on the evidence of Mr Turner, I'm afraid. Apart from his previous convictions, he has told two distinctly opposite stories. Only one on oath, that is true, but in the witness box he has refused to deny the truth of the other statement.

MR CREAMER: I'll take my client's instructions, my Lord.

But in spite of Mr Creamer's efforts, neither the plaintiff nor the defendant would agree to give way one inch. So Roger had to hear the whole of the evidence and to arrive at a conclusion.

Before the case was over he went to a cocktail party, where a woman said to him: 'Do tell me how it is you can always tell which side is telling the truth? I should have thought it was very difficult. But you wouldn't be a judge if you couldn't, would you?'

'Wouldn't I?' said Roger, with feeling. 'It's quite true that in a lot of cases, the majority, the truth does appear with reasonable certainty, and most judges, if not all of them, would decide those cases, as far as the facts are concerned, the same way. But there are cases where Judge A would believe the plaintiff and Judge B would believe the defendant, and the truth might be that they were both wrong.'

'Then you actually make mistakes?' said the woman.

'I'm afraid so,' said Roger.

'But that's dreadful,' said the woman. 'What's the point of going to law unless the judge is going to get it right?'

'Well, we usually do,' said Roger, 'I hope, but we're only human, I'm afraid, and there must be some mistakes.'

'Then it isn't justice,' said the woman. 'And what about people who are hanged and sent to prison? I'd no idea.'

'Criminal law is different,' said Roger. 'To begin with, all serious crimes are tried by a jury. There are twelve of them. And, if they think there's any doubt about the case, they always acquit.'

'But that isn't right, if the person's guilty,' said the woman. 'That isn't justice, either. Are many guilty people acquitted, d'you think?'

'Oh yes,' said Roger incautiously, 'lots. Very few others, as a matter of fact.'

'D'you mean that?' said the woman.

'I'm afraid so,' said Roger. 'In order to prevent the injustice, to which you referred, of people being hanged or imprisoned for crimes they haven't committed, we give prisoners every reasonable chance of being acquitted.'

'Then there are murderers and other criminals walking free in the streets?'

'I'm afraid so. But, don't forget, there are quite a number of criminals who are never caught, and they're walking about the streets, too.'

'Two wrongs don't make a right. Of course the police can't catch everyone. But if, when they do catch them, you let them out again – what's the good of it?'

'Well – everyone's entitled to be tried, don't you think?' said Roger.

'Certainly,' said the woman, 'but, if they're guilty, then they should be convicted, not let out to do it again.'

'But guilt has to be proved,' said Roger.

'Of course it has, and it's up to the lawyers and judges to prove it. I always had such a high opinion of English justice. You really have shaken me. What about the figure of justice on the Old Bailey? What does it stand for? Convicting the innocent and acquitting the guilty, as far as I can see.'

'I never said the innocent were convicted,' said Roger.

'But it must happen sometimes. You said yourself mistakes are made and that "we're only human".'

'Well – I suppose it does happen very occasionally.'

'That's all I said,' said the woman. 'The innocent convicted and the guilty often acquitted. That's right, isn't it? I didn't misunderstand you about that – guilty people are often acquitted?'

'Yes,' said Roger. 'I apologize, but it does happen quite often.'

'And you're a High Court judge and sometimes you decide cases the wrong way?'

'Yes, I'm afraid so. But they can always go to the Court of Appeal.'

'And are they always right?'

'No, not always,' said Roger. 'But you can sometimes appeal from them to the House of Lords.'

'And are they always right?'

'Yes,' said Roger. 'In law they are always right.'

'I don't quite know what the "in law" means, but, if they're always right, why can't we start with them? It seems much better than having a lot of judges like you – forgive my frankness – making mistakes and some more judges in the Court of Appeal making more mistakes. Why not begin in the House of Lords and make no mistakes?'

'I'm afraid that, for one thing, there aren't enough Law Lords.'

'Then make some more. They're always talking about reforming the House of Lords. But I am really most disturbed by all this. As far as I can see, there isn't much point in having judges and courts at all, if they're going to make mistakes the whole time.'

'We do get things right sometimes,' said Roger.

'How d'you know?' said the woman. 'You may be mistaken when you think you've got it right.'

Roger looked round the room to see if he could find some means of escape, but, before he could find any, his assailant went on: 'Oh, there's one thing you can tell me, if you don't mind. I know it's very stupid of me – I ought to know. Can you give a weekly servant a week's notice in the middle of a week, or must the notice end with the end of a current week?'

'Well, probably – ' began Roger.

'Probably!' interrupted the woman. 'Probably! You're a judge, aren't you? Don't you know the law?'

'Well,' began Roger apologetically, 'it isn't absolutely certain, but the better view, in my opinion, is – '

'Look, what is this?' said the woman. 'Have I done the wrong thing? Oughtn't I to ask a judge for his opinion? I suppose it's trade union rules. Doing a solicitor out of his six and eight.'

'No, it really isn't that,' said Roger. 'The truth is – '

'I thought you didn't always know the truth.'

'What I mean is,' persisted Roger, 'that it would probably be held today that a week's notice would be effective whenever it was given, but there is no definite modern authority on the subject.'

'An awful lot of words to deal with a simple point,' said the woman. 'Anyway, what would you advise a person to do?'

'Well,' said Roger, 'I'd certainly advise them to give a week's notice to expire at the end of a current week.'

'Come again,' said the woman.

Roger repeated his remark.

'But I thought you said that wasn't the law – I beg your pardon, *probably* wasn't the law.'

'Yes, I did.'

'Well – you don't seem to have the courage of your convictions, do you? Have you been a judge long? Oh – excuse me, I must go and talk to – '

And she moved away. Roger did not very much mind that he never had the opportunity of explaining that his advice was given in order to prevent the possibility of argument; better to give a few extra days than risk an action in the County Court, however likely to win you might be, he would have said.

Next morning Roger had to make up his mind about the dispute between Mr Jones and Mr Tester. In trying to decide where the truth lay, Roger could not help remembering his conversation at the cocktail party.

Who was responsible for the interference with the ice? Mr Jones said it was Mr Tester. Mr Tester said it was Mr Jones. The waiter had said that it was each of them. The question was – what was Mr Justice Thursby going to say? There was really nothing to guide him. The waiter was a self-confessed man of bad character. The plaintiff and the defendant had each had to make damaging admissions about their past conduct. For a moment Roger did say to himself – well, does it matter anyway? No one in this case is worth twopence. But then he pulled himself together and reminded himself that, if a person came to the Courts, however undeserving he might be, he was entitled to get the best decision the court was capable of giving. He was glad that his assailant at the cocktail party could not see his mind working.

In the end Roger decided that the plaintiff had not proved his case.

'It is for the plaintiff to establish,' he said, 'by a preponderance of probability, that it was the defendant who was responsible for the incident. I can find nothing in the evidence to suggest that it was more likely to have been the defendant than the plaintiff. It is true that, apart from the evidence, one would have said that it was more probable that the defendant had hatched such a comparatively simple, if unusual, plot than that the plaintiff would have gone in for such an involved one. But, having had the doubtful advantage of seeing both Mr Jones and Mr Tester in the witness box, I really cannot choose between them. Unlike Mr Turner they have no criminal convictions against them but whether that is due to luck or great care it is not necessary for me to conjecture. They have chosen to wash their dirty linen in public, but that does not seem to have made it any cleaner. I do not pretend that I know where the truth lies in this case, and all I can say is that the plaintiff has not satisfied me that it lies with him. There will accordingly be judgement for the defendant but in all the circumstances I shall make no order as to costs.'

Both sides left the court thoroughly dissatisfied with the decision. The only person who was reasonably satisfied was Mr Turner, the waiter, who had been paid by both parties and against whom there was not sufficient evidence to enable the police to prosecute for any offence.

After Roger had gone to his room the usher brought him a note. It was from Plummer: 'Can you remind me,' it said, 'whether it was tomatoes or oranges that a man once threw at the Court of Appeal?'

CHAPTER NINE

Something for Nothing

A few days later Roger was walking to the Old Bailey for his first appearance there as judge, when he was accosted by Plummer.

'I'm not getting on your nerves, I hope,' he said.

'You're a confounded nuisance,' said Roger, 'but I can't think what you get out of it. Anyway, it was tomatoes – and the man was sent to prison. And, I may add, he was a bad shot and they missed.'

'I suppose one wants practice,' said Plummer, 'at that sort of thing. What's the elevation? I must work it out.'

'You'll end up in jail, you know,' said Roger. 'I hope I don't have to send you there.'

'So do I,' said Plummer. 'It'd be so awkward for you. Well, I must be off. See you again soon. Shall I give your love to Toni?'

Roger did not answer at once. One sends love to all sorts of people. It is often a pure formality. It wouldn't be in writing, either. All the same, could he, a High Court judge, send his love to a dance hostess, even though her father was a doctor? Manifestly be seen to be – oh – damn! 'Yes,' he said.

Roger felt a little self-conscious as he took part in the ceremonial of opening the Session at the Old Bailey. He decided that he would take back to Anne the bunch of flowers which he was traditionally given, and then, confound it, he thought how nice it would be to give a bunch to Toni. This was multiplication with a vengeance. Of course, he wouldn't dream of doing such a thing. A little girl of twenty-three, whom he'd met once and who worked in a night club. Never heard of such a thing.

'I beg your pardon, Mr Summers?' he said to Counsel, who had apparently been addressing him.

'My Lord,' said Counsel, 'the facts in this case are as follows. About six months ago an advertisement appeared in a sporting newspaper to the following effect: "Help me exploit my new system. Results guaranteed. Send £10 cash for a share. Smith, Box 1713." The advertisement was not very different from those of many other tipsters, and no one answered it. The next week another advertisement appeared from the same source. "Last week we backed three winners at 3 to 1, 5 to 2, and 6 to 4, and one loser (4th at 20 to 1). We only made just over £250 as we hadn't the necessary capital. Proof this paper. Send £10 for a share next week." Mr Smith produced to the paper in question his bookmaker's account, showing that he had indeed backed the horses in question and received a cheque for the amount referred to. As a result of the advertisement a few people sent £10 each and a few more sent £5 for a half-share. They all received their money back with the following letter: "Dear Sir, Thank you for your letter and enclosure, which I regret having to return as I was over-capitalized for the week. I hope that I may be able to let you share in the new system on a later occasion. Yours sincerely, H Smith." The following week the advertisement read as follows. "We apologize to those whose money we were unable to accept. And we sympathize. Last week we backed four winners, 10 to 1, 5 to 1, 6 to 4 and even money, and NO losers. Proof this paper." Again Mr Smith had produced to the newspaper his bookmaker's account proving his claim to be correct. In consequence of this advertisement quite a number of people sent in their money. It was all returned to them with a similar note to the first one, but adding: "I am hoping that in the not too distant future I shall be in a position to land a really big coup at startling odds and I shall need your money for this purpose. I cannot, of course, be quite sure when this is going to be, and naturally I cannot advertise it directly or the odds may shorten." The next week there was a similar advertisement showing the tremendous success of the system, which was again proved to the satisfaction of the newspaper in the usual way. This went on until the public were figuratively hammering at Mr Smith's Box number, and begging to be allowed to subscribe to his system and to buy a share in the gold mine. Time after time Mr Smith hardened his heart and refused to accept anyone's money. But eventually he relented and was kind enough to accept 1,000 offers, accompanied by £10 in cash. Each of the investors waited expectantly for the registered letter which was to bring them their winnings. It was obviously pretty well a certainty. There could be no doubt about it. The sporting paper which carried the advertisement was a thoroughly reputable paper, and "proof this paper" meant what it said. There was no reason why a system which had succeeded week after week should suddenly fail. So each waited for the registered letter. And, when it never came, they looked in the paper to see what the advertisement would say. It said nothing, because there was no advertisement. They started to write to Mr Smith at the Box number, to enquire what had happened, but they had no answer. Then they wrote to the newspaper, which at once started to make enquiries for Mr Smith. But he was not to be found – neither he nor the £10,000 which had been sent him. The address which he had given to the newspaper was an accommodation address belonging to a newsagent. All the newsagent could say was that a bearded man with dark glasses used to call for the letters. So the newspaper made enquiries from Mr Smith's bookmaker. They had no answer from that source either. They then made enquiries about the bookmaker and they found that it was a small limited company which had been formed a few months before Mr Smith had started to insert his advertisements. It didn't take the investigators long to realize that Mr Smith had been his own bookmaker and sent himself his winning accounts. The police were informed and they made a search for Mr Smith. Eventually they found him, and here he is, my Lord. He has pleaded guilty to ten counts of obtaining money by false pretences, but the total amount involved is, as I told your Lordship, ten thousand pounds.'

Counsel then called the police officer in charge of the case, who gave a short account of the prisoner's past history, and Roger then asked Mr Smith if he had anything to say in mitigation of sentence.

'Although it is a first offence,' Roger said, 'you will have to go to prison. The question is, for how long?'

'My Lord,' said the prisoner, 'if it weren't for people's greed, things like this would never happen. Everyone wants something for nothing, and then they grumble when they don't get it.' He paused.

'Anything else?' said Roger.

'Well, my Lord,' he added, 'I did send them back their money each time – except the last.'

'But you wouldn't have made anything like so much if you hadn't. It was worth it, wasn't it?' said Roger.

'I don't know, my Lord,' said the prisoner. 'That depends on you.'

CHAPTER TEN

The Motor Mower

If Roger had known that Plummer was preparing a further assault on him, he would have felt less comfortable when he sat for the first time as Judge in Chambers. The 'Judge in Chambers' has to deal mostly with the various applications which are made in the course of an action. While Roger was dealing with a number of such matters, Plummer was talking to Toni.

'I think perhaps,' he said, 'that we should use you again.'

'That suits me fine,' said Toni. 'I like my judge. Can't see too much of him. Pity he's married.'

'Good,' said Plummer. 'I must see how to bring the young people together.'

While Plummer was considering this problem, Roger was beginning to hear an application in a case about a motor mower.

'This is an appeal from a decision of Master Banger, my Lord,' began Mr Twine of Counsel. 'The learned Master refused to order the plaintiff to deliver particulars of his statement of claim.'

'What is the action about?' said Roger.

'It's a claim for damages in respect of the sale of a motor mowing machine which my clients, the defendants, sold to the plaintiff, my Lord. He complains that it makes all sorts of odd, and sometimes vulgar patterns on his lawn. We want particulars of each oddity and vulgarity relied upon.'

'Can't the machine be adjusted?' asked Roger. 'It seems a bit absurd to have litigation on the subject.'

'Exactly what my clients said and say,' said Mr Twine.

'Really!' said Mr Twine's opponent, Mr Groaner. 'I'm amazed at my friend saying that. We've begged and begged the defendants to come and adjust the machine.'

'Each time my clients have called,' replied Mr Twine, 'there's been nobody in.'

'Well,' said Roger, 'is it too late now? Mightn't it be better for an appointment to be made now, so that there need be no oddities or vulgarities on the plaintiff's lawn in the future, rather than for an enquiry of doubtful value being made into the oddities and vulgarities of the past? Though I must confess,' he added, 'I'm a little intrigued to know what they were.'

'My Lord,' said Mr Groaner, 'I can satisfy your Lordship's curiosity. Here are some photographs.'

'This is an application for particulars,' said Mr Twine. 'His Lordship isn't trying the action. I don't know what the photographs have got to do with it.'

'Well, they might constitute the particulars, mightn't they?' said Roger.

'If my learned friend will limit his complaints to the photographs, I should be quite satisfied, my Lord.'

'Well, Mr Groaner,' said Roger, 'are you prepared to rely solely on the photographs?'

'Not at this stage, my Lord,' said Mr Groaner.

'My learned friend wants it both ways,' complained Mr Twine. 'He won't limit his particulars to the photographs and at the same time he wants to prejudice your Lordship by showing them to you. My clients have no knowledge of them whatever – they may have been taken anywhere as far as my clients know. They ought to have been asked to be present when they were taken.'

'They were,' said Mr Groaner.

'They were not,' said Mr Twine.

'Well,' said Roger, 'you can't both be right. Anyway, let me see the photographs.'

Mr Groaner handed them to Roger, and the clerk leaned slightly to one side so that he could see them too.

'They are rather extraordinary,' said Roger, 'but I'm not quite clear where the vulgarity comes in.'

'Well, my Lord,' said Mr Groaner, 'if your Lordship takes photograph number one and holds it upside down – '

'Really,' commented Mr Twine, 'perhaps my friend has an X-ray apparatus as well.'

'If your Lordship will be good enough to look at photograph number one upside down …' repeated Mr Groaner.

'No, I don't think so,' said Roger, restraining his natural curiosity very creditably. 'I should probably miss the point anyway. However, Mr Groaner, if you won't limit your complaints to what is shown on the photographs, why shouldn't you give particulars of everything you do complain about?'

'My Lord,' said Mr Groaner, 'surely I can't be expected to say in what position every blade of grass lay after the machine had been over it? That was the Master's view, my Lord, and he is, if I may say so, a very experienced Masters.'

'I'm afraid', said Roger, 'that I've always deprecated the threatening of new judges in chambers with the names and experiences of Master.'

'Oh, my Lord, I wasn't doing anything of the sort. I shouldn't dream of – '

'Very well,' said Roger, 'I must have misunderstood you. The appeal will be allowed and the particulars as asked for must be delivered in fourteen days. Unless, of course, both parties are sensible enough to put their heads together and settle the whole dispute by putting the machine right.'

'But who's to pay the costs, my Lord?' asked Mr Groaner.

'Who's to pay them when the action's been fought, Mr Groaner?' said Roger. 'It may be the plaintiff or it may be the defendant, or it may be both of them, but, whoever it is, the costs will then be ten times as much as they are now.'

Roger completed the order, and Mr Twine and Mr Groaner gave place to Mr Bone and Mr Streak. Outside the judge's room Mr Twine, flushed with victory, ventured his opinion to Mr Groaner that Roger was going to be jolly good, with which opinion Mr Groaner, smarting with defeat, profoundly disagreed.

CHAPTER ELEVEN

The Soft Shoe Club

Roger had always found time very kind to him when he walked down Bond Street. That is to say that, after his eyes had strayed in the way to which Henry had referred, although a feeling of regret that he could not follow his inclinations sometimes assailed him, it did not last long and, within a few minutes or at the most half an hour or so, it was all over. So, when some months had passed without his seeing Toni again, the various emotions which she had stirred in him had pretty well died down. Then, one day, a judge, who was much older than he was but whom he knew quite well, asked him to come and see him in his room.

'Ah, Roger,' said Mr Justice Breeze, 'nice of you to come.'

Mr Justice Breeze was a very cheerful bachelor. He did not pretend to be a good lawyer nor, indeed, a particularly good judge, but he dealt out rough and ready justice with robust good humour. When at the Bar he had been almost irresistible to juries. His smiling red face and his down-to-earth, boisterous speeches, full of colloquialisms, jollied the jury along with him. When he went on the Bench he retained very much the same manner, though he toned it down a little. Counsel in his Court knew that it was no use relying on the finer points. Mr Justice Breeze was going to take the broad view and he intensely disliked technical points.

'That's a mean little point, Mr Jones,' he would say. 'You know what I'd like to tell you to do with that. Abandon it. Hasn't your client any merits? I'm sure such a jovial-looking man must have some. Take fresh instructions, Mr Jones,' he would add. 'Tell your client not to skulk in the nasty, mean little street he's wandered down and to come out into the broad, open highway of justice.'

He often got his way, though not always, but, when he did, he was frequently reversed in the Court of Appeal. Not that he cared. He had given a decision which was just in his view, and, if the lawyers above him chose to alter it, that was their business.

'I was upheld again the other day,' he once remarked to a friend. 'I must be losing my grip.'

Why he had remained a bachelor sometimes puzzled even him. He was a normal man, with normal instincts, but he had never had a love affair, unhappy or otherwise. Marriage had simply passed him by. At one time, in his younger days, he had been very much in demand by mothers of eligible daughters. He had been a double Blue, was ruggedly good-looking, and was obviously doing well at the Bar. But it just never happened. Possibly he was too bluff and too hearty. The broad, open highway of justice was all right in the Courts, but at home technicalities and refinements have their place.

'I've had an invitation,' said Breeze, 'and I wondered if you and your wife would care to come with me. I'm not much used to these places.'

'Oh?' said Roger enquiringly. 'It's very nice of you.'

'I'll tell you what it is. A girl, a dancer or something, broke or sprained her ankle at one of these clubs and she's brought an action against her employers. She claims that the floor was unusually slippery and various other things about the platform where she had to perform, and so on. They want me to see the place. They offered me an evening's entertainment and asked if I'd like to bring a friend or a couple of friends. Well, in view of my celibate state and the gossip column reporters, I thought I'd take a couple of friends. We can choose any night. What about it?'

Roger did not answer for a moment. He was puzzled. Here was a judge trying a case between the proprietors of a club and an employee and the judge was actually going to accept hospitality from the owners of the club. It seemed odd to Roger, very odd indeed. If a judge accepted a favour from one party to litigation either side might think he had been influenced by the fact. If he decided for the person who did him the service the other party might feel aggrieved; if he decided the other way it might be thought that the judge had deliberately decided against the person doing him the favour, to show how fair he was.

Breeze apparently sensed what Roger was thinking.

'Don't look so puzzled,' he said. 'Both sides want me to come. Counsel for the plaintiff was quite upset when I suggested that I couldn't very well accept hospitality from the defendants. He begged me to come and said that, if I didn't, I shouldn't be able to follow the plaintiff's case properly. I saw them in my private room. They're going to be there too, and both of them pressed me to come. Apparently they both agree that, unless one sees the place as it is when guests are there and so on, you can't see the point of the case. Well, I don't suppose I shall see the point anyway, if it's as difficult as that, but I don't mind trying on the terms suggested. Might be quite amusing. Haven't been to one of those places for years.'

'Well, it's very nice of you,' said Roger. 'I think Anne and

I would love it. Is there much in the case? Is it a permanent injury?'

'Oh, no,' said Breeze. 'It's not really serious.'

'Well, it's very odd spending so much money on the case. Anyway, why didn't they bring it in the County Court?'

'I asked them that,' said Breeze, 'and, what's more, I warned them of the consequences of trying the action in the High Court. Neither side seemed to mind in the least.'

'Are their counsel any good?' asked Roger.

'Oh, yes, both of them. They know what they're up to. That's why I didn't say any more.'

'Well, I must just ask Anne, but I'm sure we'd love it. What's the name of the club, by the way?'

'Some odd name. I forget. No, I've got it. The Soft Shoe Club. Heaven knows what that means.'

'Plummer!' said Roger.

'What's that?'

Roger thought for a moment. Then all he said was: 'I know the chap who runs it. He was at school with me.' He had been about to warn Breeze about Plummer's activities, and then he suddenly realized that, if he did so, he might be prejudicing the judge who was trying the action by giving him private information unknown to either side. Unless, therefore, Plummer really started to do something, he decided he would say nothing about him, at any rate until after the action had been decided. Having got over that hurdle Roger realized, not without some pleasure, that he would be seeing Toni again.

When he got home that evening he said to Anne: 'We've had an invitation.'

'Oh?'

'To go to the Soft Shoe Club.'

'What!' said Anne. 'You're not serious?'

'It's quite all right,' said Roger. 'Plummer didn't ask me.' He then told Anne how the invitation arose.

'It would be quite fun, wouldn't it?' he said almost casually.

Anne hesitated for a moment. She was going to agree to the suggestion and the only question in her mind was in what form she should do so. If she said – 'Yes, of course we'll go,' that would at once indicate to Roger that she wasn't really keen on the idea herself but would go to please him. If she said – 'All right,' or 'Yes, certainly,' it would have much the same effect. On the other hand, if she said, with obvious enthusiasm, 'Yes, let's, it'll be great fun to break out for a bit,' it would not be true. She was not a jealous woman, but she had not been altogether sorry when Roger had ceased to mention Toni's name. She was not in the least frightened that Roger would lose his head if he saw her again; they were entirely happy in every sense of the word and nothing could come between them; moreover, as Roger had more than once explained to her, there were certain things – quite a number – which a judge mustn't do; and Roger, who had always been virtuous to the point of priggishness, was not going to fling over the traces now; fling over the traces! What a ridiculous thought; he wouldn't even do anything mildly silly; what more natural than that he should want to see Toni again? She was apparently a most attractive girl. Anyway it would be a good thing for her to see what she was up against. Up against! How ridiculous. She really must take hold of herself. And perhaps it would be better to see this Toni, not to have to wonder – to wonder – but the moment was up; if she let it go on any longer Roger would assume that she didn't want to go.

'What a lovely idea,' she said, 'It'll be fun to break out

for once.'

'You're wonderful, Anne,' said Roger. 'What a bit of luck you're such a bad driver.'

So a day was fixed for the party and, when it arrived, Roger went to Court in a very happy frame of mind. What an incredibly lucky man he was. A High Court judge at the age of forty-six and a perfect wife whom he adored. And today he was going to see again the most attractive girl he had ever met – apart from Anne, of course.

Roger was always courteous on the Bench, but he was particularly friendly that day.

'He's going to be like Hathaway,' said one counsel to another. He was referring to a judge who was so extremely good-natured that he almost apologized in his judgements to the party against whom he decided. He certainly said everything nice he could about someone who was going to lose his case. It was not long before the Bar realized this and counsel for the plaintiff, for example, would hear with much regret Hathaway J say, early in his judgement: 'Now, the plaintiff is plainly an honest man, and I have no doubt whatever but that he came here to tell me what in his heart he believes to be the truth.'

That preamble meant that in due course Hathaway J was going to reject everything the plaintiff said in favour of what the defendant said. Or, if the case depended on a point of law, Mr X would know the game was up if the judgement contained sentences like this: 'Now, Mr X has argued with great skill and determination that the words used could not in law amount to a warranty. I am most grateful to Mr X for the great help he has given me and, if it is not impertinent of me to say so, his argument on the matter was as powerful and clear an argument as I have heard for a long time.'

If Mr X appeared for the plaintiff, he would at once start

to endorse his brief with 'Judgement for the Defendant'.

Even when addressing a hardened criminal before sentence, he would use words of apology. On one occasion, for example, he said: 'George Smith, you have, I am afraid, been convicted by the jury of what I cannot avoid describing as a most serious crime. Moreover, it is unfortunately the case that you already have several convictions for the same kind of crime, and the present offence was committed very shortly after your release from your last sentence. I am sure you will understand that it is my duty to protect the public from – ' (he was going to say 'people like you' but, realizing the offence this might give, he changed it just in time to) 'from being knocked down and robbed. I am sure you will appreciate that. One must be able to walk down the road without fear of being attacked, in what some people might describe as a somewhat cowardly way, from behind with a bludgeon. In all the circumstances and bearing in mind everything that your learned counsel has said – if he will allow me to say so – so very ably on your behalf, the least sentence that I can pass on you for this offence is twelve years' imprisonment.'

'Twelve years!' said the prisoner dumbly.

'I'm afraid so,' said Hathaway J.

'But I only got half a crown off her.'

'But wasn't that mere chance? I suspect that you would have taken more if she'd had more. And you did hit her over the head with a bludgeon, you know, didn't you? No, I'm afraid I can't alter my decision.'

'I'll appeal.'

'Of course you can appeal and – ' but the next words stuck in Hathaway's throat. He had been about to say that no one would be more pleased than he if the Court of Criminal Appeal reduced the sentence, when he realized that the prisoner deserved every day of his sentence for a cruel and wicked crime. So Hathaway J contented himself with substituting for words a friendly smile, as the prisoner was taken away.

'Cor,' he said to one of the warders, 'give me old Bouncing Bill any day.'

He was referring to a judge who delivered long and fierce homilies to criminals on whom he was about to pass judgement, but followed up the words with an exceptionally light sentence.

'This', he had been heard to say, 'is one of the worst cases I have known. I repeat, one of the worst cases I have ever known. It has no redeeming features whatever. You are a coward and a bully and you are extremely lucky that you are not charged with murder. That is no fault of yours. The man you struck might well have died. He owes his life to no mercy shown by you. There was no provocation of any kind and you haven't even the excuse that you were drunk. You have made things worse by pleading not guilty and putting up a perjured defence of an alibi, which the jury rightly rejected. If it were not for your previous good character, I should sentence you to imprisonment for life.'

At this stage those who did not know Bouncing Bill expected a sentence of anything from five to fifteen years, though five would have seemed a bathos. 'As it is,' the judge went on, 'the least sentence I can pass upon you for a dastardly crime like this is twelve' – (the prisoner went white) – 'months imprisonment.' (The prisoner fainted.)

'Cor,' repeated Mr Smith, after having been sentenced by Hathaway J, 'you don't have to listen to the words, but you have to do the sentence. Twelve years for half a crown!'

'Lucky it wasn't five bob, chum,' said the warder.

Roger rose from Court in the same good spirits in which

he started the day. It seemed a long time between 4.30pm when he left the Law Courts and 9.30pm, the time they were to meet at the Soft Shoe Club. But, by reading bits in the evening papers which he never normally read, and some of the advertisements, Roger helped to make it pass and he was delighted when he looked at the clock and saw that it was time to start.

'You'll make yourself sore,' said Anne, after Roger's electric razor had seemed to her to be buzzing for hours.

'Is that all right?' asked Roger, presenting his smooth face for inspection.

'Beautiful, darling.'

'But you didn't feel it,' said Roger.

Anne took his face in both her hands.

'You could kiss anyone with that face,' she said, as she let him go.

'I've no intention of kissing anyone,' said Roger.

'Not even me?' asked Anne.

It was a gala night at the Club. According to the parties it had been a gala night when the accident took place. There was a special floor show and there seemed to be a legal flavour about a good deal of it. Even the first crooner, a girl with a lazy, husky voice, sang a song about Love Limited, a company which had only issued two shares, one for me and one for you. She dealt at some length with the memorandum and articles of association of the company. There was a line which ended in 'Wore 'em' in order to rhyme with quorum, and a quorum consisted of two, that is to say, me and you, and the lady added that she didn't *care* if at a meeting the quorum filled the only *chair*.

Then came a troupe of girls dressed in barristers' wigs and bands and very little else, who sang a chorus the words of which, mercifully, Roger thought, could not be heard. And then another girl came and sang a song, the last line of each verse of which was: 'But I'm no judge.' Needless to say, she turned to the judges' table whenever she said it.

It was just after this turn that Toni came up to their table, looking dazzling. Roger introduced her to Anne and to Breeze, who, after she had gone, asked Roger: 'Was she at school with you, too?'

Roger explained, without going into detail, how he had met her.

'You seem to get around a bit,' said Breeze. 'That's the advantage of being married. You can do all sorts of things that I can't.'

'I thought it was the other way round,' said Roger.

During the evening counsel on each side explained to Breeze how, according to their respective views of the case, the accident had happened. While they were doing so, Roger danced with Toni. He had already danced twice with Anne.

'So you really are a judge,' said Toni, as they danced. 'I thought Plummer might have been pulling a fast one on me. I'll pull one on him one of these days.'

'No, I am a judge, I'm afraid,' said Roger.

'Don't apologize,' said Toni. 'Someone has to be. It does cramp your style a bit, though,' she added.

'Well,' said Roger, 'I suppose it does. But that's just as well.'

At that moment a photographer took a picture of them.

'There's one for my album,' said Toni. 'Will you sign it for me?'

'I'm afraid not,' said Roger.

'Frightened I might forge your signature later?'

'Of course not.'

'Well, what is it? You're almost as stern as you are on the Bench – worse, really. I came to Court the other day and saw you. When you seem to look at people in the Court – the public, I mean – are you really looking at them? I thought you looked straight at me.'

'I did,' said Roger.

'Were you pleased I came?'

'Yes, of course.'

'Why?'

'Oh, I don't know. It's nice to have the look of the Court improved by someone like you coming in.'

'Then any pretty girl would have done?'

'I didn't say so,' said Roger.

Toni waited a moment before going on, and then: 'Isn't that the sort of answer some witnesses give?' she asked.

Roger laughed.

'Quite right, but how do you know?'

'One learns quite a lot in this job. But oughtn't you to have been thinking about the case, not about people in the Court?'

'I was,' said Roger, 'but that doesn't prevent one noticing people coming in and out.'

'Tell me something else,' said Toni. 'Sending people to prison; what does it feel like?'

'Well, I haven't sent many, so far, but I can't say that I felt very much at the time. It's just one's job. Like an undertaker's. Of course, if we can avoid sending people to prison most of us do.'

'Makes you enjoy your lunch or dinner better?'

'No, that isn't a fair way of putting it at all. We do try to do the right thing. I dare say we fail sometimes, or often if you like, but we do try. I certainly wouldn't give a man another chance because I should enjoy dancing with you more in the evening if I did.'

'How do you enjoy it?'

'Very much.'

'Will you come again?'

'I shouldn't think so,' said Roger, 'but that isn't because I haven't enjoyed it. It's just one of the disadvantages of my job.'

'Then,' said Toni, 'if you weren't a judge would you come and dance with me more often?'

'Certainly, if I weren't married.'

'But you are.'

'I know. Very happily.'

'Then being a judge has nothing to do with it.'

'Well, it's both,' said Roger. 'A judge shouldn't be seen regularly at night clubs and, apart from that, you're much too attractive for a married man to see a lot of.'

'What a shame,' said Toni. 'I wore this dress for you.'

'It's charming,' said Roger. 'If ever you think of changing your job, and you want an introduction to a doctor, Anne and I will be very pleased to help you.'

'Anne and you?'

'Yes – Anne and I.'

'And, if I became a doctor's receptionist, would I see more of you then?'

'Well, you'd see me if I came to the doctor.'

'What complaint do you think you're most likely to suffer from? Then I'll know the sort of doctor to choose.'

'I'm very well at the moment.'

'What do judges mostly suffer from? Jaundice?'

When the dance was over, Toni went with Roger back to his table.

'You know,' she announced to them all, 'it didn't really feel any different from dancing with anyone else.'

'If you'd been dancing with me,' said Breeze, 'it would have felt different all right.'

'In what way?' asked Toni.

'Well,' said Breeze, 'I used to play forward at rugger, and everyone says that I dance like it.'

'I'd love to find out,' said Toni.

Breeze got up.

'At your own risk, young woman,' he said, 'you may. But no damages, mind you, if I kick your shin and stand on your toes.'

'I'm sure you dance beautifully,' said Toni.

'Well,' said Breeze, 'something learned is something gained. Come along.' And he and Toni took the floor. At that moment one of the counsel engaged in the case asked Anne to dance, and Roger was left to himself. He sought out Plummer.

'What's all this in aid of?' he asked him.

'Her Majesty's judges,' said Plummer.

'You've something up your sleeve,' said Roger. 'What is it?'

'You're not in Court now,' said Plummer. 'I can refuse to answer here. But I'll tell you, if you like.'

'Well?' said Roger.

'You won't pass it on, old boy, of course.'

'Provided there's nothing illegal about it, I won't,' said Roger. 'But if there is, I may have to.'

'No,' said Plummer, 'there's nothing illegal, as far as I can see. But I don't want everyone to do the same thing. So keep it to yourself.'

'Well,' said Roger, 'what's it all about?'

'D'you know how much it costs to advertise for three minutes on commercial TV?'

'No,' said Roger, 'but I know it's a lot.'

'And half a page in a daily paper, that's a pretty good price, too.'

'Well?'

'The law is cheaper, my dear boy, that's all.'

'What d'you mean?' said Roger. 'Is this action just a fake to get advertisement?'

'No and yes,' said Plummer. 'Of course it's not a fake. That would mean perjury, contempt of Court, conspiracy and I don't know what. No conscientious objection to any of 'em, old boy, but very inconvenient to be found out. Oh dear no, the action's genuine enough. The poor girl sprained her ankle all right. So I suddenly had a bright idea. Make a case of it. There are always a few celebrities here. Call them as witnesses. If you can, get the judge to come and see the place in action. Keep the evidence as interesting as possible. I sent her to a good firm of solicitors. Of course I'll pay her costs, win or lose, and she'll get any damages she recovers. The whole thing won't cost me more than six hundred pounds, and, properly managed, I'll get more than five times that in advertising. The papers tomorrow will have some quite nice photographs, and when the case comes on again there'll be more and lots of publicity. The girl may give an interview on TV and so forth and so on. Now, what's wrong with that?'

Roger thought for a moment.

'It might be said to be an abuse of the process of the Court,' he said, after a pause.

'Why?' said Plummer. 'The girl sprained her ankle, didn't she? She did it while doing her job. I may be responsible or I may not. Why shouldn't she sue me, and, if she does, why should I pay unless the Court says I'm liable? And why shouldn't a decent employer pay his employee's costs? It's quite true that that isn't the real object of the exercise. But then what about libel actions? They're brought to advertise sometimes, aren't they?'

'I see your point,' said Roger. 'You ought to have gone to the Bar instead of the Army.'

'Don't,' said Plummer. 'I might have become like you, or old bone shaker. Look at him there. There's one person who's glad the action was brought. I'll have to give Toni a new pair of shoes – and a new back, too, I should think.'

Breeze J certainly appeared to be enjoying himself, though it looked as though he could have done with more room for manoeuvre.

'And if we serve it up with just a little bit of embroidery here and there,' continued Plummer, 'well, there's no harm in that.'

'Embroidery?' queried Roger.

'Well,' said Plummer, 'all I mean is that we shan't ask the witnesses to be as boring as possible. Pop in anything that'll look good in the papers. We're lucky in the judge, too. He's always good news value. We might have had you.'

'Oh, no,' said Roger. 'I should have refused to try it, as I know you.'

'Suppose we knew all the judges, what would happen then?'

'Well, if it were absolutely necessary, they'd appoint a Commissioner specially to try the case. You couldn't know every barrister who'd be competent to try it.'

'Shouldn't want to, old boy,' said Plummer. 'But it's a good way of getting out of being tried by a particular judge. Ask him to tea.'

'He might not come,' said Roger.

'Oh, dear,' said Plummer. 'You don't change, do you? In words of one syllable, let me explain. There are ways and means of asking a particular judge to tea. And I don't necessarily mean tea. It might be supper or drinks or what have you. One can usually find someone who knows someone who knows someone who knows the chap you want. Then just arrange it.'

He stopped for a moment.

'If I were up at the Old Bailey,' he went on, 'there are certainly one or two judges I'd ask to tea.'

'You'd better start,' said Roger. 'It looks as though you'll find yourself there one day.'

'Can I call you to give evidence of good character?' said Plummer.

Eventually the evening ended and there was unanimity among the judges about the success of the evening at the Soft Shoe Club.

'I could do with a few more cases like this,' said Breeze to Roger as they left. 'What's that young lady's name?'

Roger told him.

'It's really "Dora Stokes",' he added.

'You seem to know a lot about her. Known her long?'

'No,' said Roger, 'I just happened to meet her through Plummer.'

'You happened to have been extremely lucky,' said Breeze.

On the way home Anne asked Roger what he thought of Toni on closer acquaintance.

'She's too attractive,' said Roger, 'but somehow I don't think I shall be finding her a job as a doctor's receptionist. I think she's quite capable of looking after herself.'

Meanwhile Plummer was questioning Toni.

'What have you arranged with your judge?' he asked.

'Well,' said Toni, 'I think I've handled the situation quite competently. But actually one can't rush the man.'

'Well, keep at him,' said Plummer. 'I can't think why his virtue still annoys me so much. But it does. And you're the answer. Now, if we can get him to take you out one evening all by yourself, we'd be getting somewhere.'

'A girl like me,' said Toni, 'always gets her judge.'

CHAPTER TWELVE

The Case of the Two Ushers

Whether it was meeting Toni again or mere coincidence, the Lord Chief Justice again appeared in Roger's dreams that night, and this time for much longer.

'I was telling you', the Chief said, 'that I always use a pin myself. I remember once, I was sitting in the Court of Criminal Appeal when the same thing happened to all of us. It caused quite a sensation. There were five of us at the time. There'd been a disagreement on the first hearing, and I'd ordered a rehearing with a court of five. Well, Counsel for the appellant, a very young man who required encouragement (you know how they get it in our Court), opened the appeal by saying rather tentatively that he had a rather unusual application to make.

' "Don't let that worry you, Mr Crape," I said in my bluff, hearty manner. "We like new suggestions in this Court. Helps to keep us on our toes, stops us becoming too hidebound. Let's hear your unusual application." And the next thing we knew was that we each of us had a girl on his knee. Naturally, as I had encouraged the young man, I did not want to rebuff him too hastily. It wouldn't have been fair. So I contented myself with saying: "Exactly what is this in aid of, Mr Crape?"

' "Your Lordships," said Mr Crape.

'I waited a moment or two but, as he remained silent, I said: "Yes, Mr Crape – go on."

' "Go on yourself," said the young lady on my knee.

' "Silence," said the usher.

'Now, that raised a nice point which, so far as I know, has never been decided in any of the books. It has been plainly laid down that an usher may not silence the judge, not even if he goes on far too long or makes a series of incredibly bad jokes. That was decided as long ago as the Queen against Willgo and Blanket. In that case an usher, whose son was at the Bar and was being prevented from arguing a case by the constant interruptions of the judge, pretended to see someone in the gallery creating a disturbance whenever the judge intervened. He did this so often that eventually the judge had to send for another usher to keep the first usher quiet. But unfortunately the new usher was an uncle by marriage of the young barrister, and he, too, began to see disturbances at the back of the gallery. So, according to the report:

'THE JUDGE: But, really, Mr Spink, that argument has been raised –

'1ST USHER: Silence in Court.

'THE JUDGE: Be quiet.

'2ND USHER: Silence.

'THE JUDGE: You, too.

'1ST USHER: Silence.

'THE JUDGE: This is really too bad.

'2ND USHER: Silence.

'Both ushers were indicted for contempt of Court, the matter being too serious to be dealt with summarily. But the difficulty was to obtain an usher at the Central Criminal Court. Although there was no actual trade union of ushers, they all stood together and refused to take part in the proceedings. Eventually the only solution was for a spare judge to act as usher. They chose a County Court judge whose presence could be most easily spared from the Bench, and the experiment was so successful that they made his deputy a judge and kept the judge on as usher, the duties of which he discharged admirably. Which makes one wonder whether it wouldn't be a good idea to repeat the process. There are one or two judges who would really make much better ushers and it would save the Court of Appeal a lot of trouble. But let me continue with The Queen against Willgo and Blanket. The judge there directed the jury as follows: "Gentlemen of the Jury" (there were no ladies in those days – on the jury, I mean), "some of you may think that I have gone on too long" (a murmured "never" from the judge-usher), "but justice could not be administered in this country if judges were prevented from going on for as long as they liked. You are not bound to listen. You have sworn to try the case according to the evidence, not the judge's version of it. Moreover, I'm sure you will understand that, if ushers were allowed to silence judges every time they made a mistake, or went on too long, or unnecessarily interrupted, the vocation of usher would be almost as important as that of the judge and the country could not bear the expense of the additional salary which would be demanded. Indeed, the usher would very soon be more important than the judge, and the ranks of the ushers would be filled by promotion from the House of Lords. Then they would start to acquire new titles. 'One of Her Majesty's Ushers learned in the Law,' for example, though QU looks odd and is a little difficult to say. So you see, gentlemen of the jury, the thing won't work. And it is your duty to convict these two men Willgo and Blanket if you are satisfied that they really intended to silence the judge. Of course, if you believe that they thought there was some disturbance in the gallery each time they said 'silence', you will acquit them. But, though it is entirely a matter for you, gentlemen of the jury, and you will completely disregard my opinion, if you think I have unwittingly expressed one, in preference for your own, the coincidences which are involved, if the story told on behalf of the prisoners is right, are surely beyond human belief. We have the record of what the learned judge was trying to say. Almost every other word was punctuated by one or other usher with a stern 'silence'. Was that word uttered because of some disturbance in the gallery, or because of a very intelligible (albeit lamentable) desire to help the young barrister whose relatives they were? And it may not be altogether without significance, gentlemen of the jury, to point out to you that, the case itself not involving any reference to murder or brutality of any kind, nor any matrimonial misconduct nor even casual immorality, the gallery was empty at the time. Of course, gentlemen of the jury, it is possible, not, you may think, likely, but possible, that each usher, looking up at the empty gallery, genuinely imagined that he saw or heard some disturbance there, but that each should make so many mistakes, and only when the judge was speaking and never when counsel was speaking, is surely beyond the bounds of even your credulity. But, I repeat, although no sane person could possibly believe the story told on behalf of the accused, it is for you to form your own opinion, unaffected by anything I have said on the matter. Will you kindly consider your verdict. It should not take you long."

'The jury, without leaving the box, returned a verdict of not guilty. The cheering which broke out was immediately suppressed by the jury itself, which, unknown to the prosecution, consisted entirely of ushers. But, although the two accused in that case were acquitted, the summing-up of the judge has stood the test of years and has never been unfavourably commented on. It can, therefore, be taken as settled law that an usher may not silence the judge himself. But unfortunately in that case there was no lady on the knee of the judge. Now, there can be no doubt that the decision that an usher may not silence the judge implicitly prevents him from silencing any appendage of the judge. Should his boots be squeaking, for example, or his deaf-aid make noises, it will be as much contempt for an usher to cry "silence" as it would be to silence the Judge's sneeze, cough, or laughter. But what about a living entity which, though nearly as close to the judge as his clothes, has a separate existence? A suggestion that at once occurred to me was that, if the noise from the lady was deliberately provoked by the judge – by a pinch, for example, or a tickle – the noise could be said in law to be the judge's, on the principle of *qui facit per aliam facit per se*. Personally, I should have been prepared to hold that it would be contempt by an usher to repress a lady's squeak, if it had been deliberately provoked by the judge. But what shall we say of what I may call an independent squeak by the lady, not judicially provoked? That is a far more difficult matter. On the whole, however, I would say, speaking for myself and not without hesitation, and recognizing that another judge might come to an entirely different conclusion – speaking for myself, I would have been prepared to say that there was sufficient identification of the judge with the lady, *if the Judge placed her on his knee himself*, to make a silencing of the lady equivalent to a silencing of the judge and to constitute contempt. But that, of course, didn't decide the question, because in that case we had not brought the ladies with us. They had, as it were, been wished on us by counsel. And that raised a further difficulty. I must confess – between you and me – and I'm sure you won't let it go any further – that the young lady on my knee was very personable, very personable indeed, and, apart from the fact that there was an audience, I'm bound to say that the situation was not without its intriguing side. And so the question arose – did it make any difference whether the judge liked the experience or not? For example, I could see my brother, Scales, who was a pronounced anti-feminist, writhing with fury, while my brother Twine seemed to be enjoying himself (if I may use the vernacular) no end. I may describe myself as being somewhere between the two. As I have said, I found the young lady attractive and the situation not without its reward but, on the other hand, I had to uphold the dignity of my position, and I did not find that altogether easy. Now, it was my young lady who squeaked. No one except me knew that it was my fault and that, by an almost unconscious act of mischief, I had – very gently, of course – used a pin. Obviously I couldn't admit it to the usher. Therefore, the squeak must be assumed in law not to have been judicially provoked. We solved the difficulty in that case by declaring the Court closed, and the rest of the proceedings were heard *in camera*. You will, of course, understand that that does not mean that pictures were taken.'

CHAPTER THIRTEEN

The Case of Mr Mowler

A few days later Roger was asked to sit in the Court of Criminal Appeal. That Court has sometimes been the subject matter of criticism both by the Bar and in Parliament. Roger himself had had experience of it in his earlier days at the Bar which made him determined that, if ever he became a judge and sat in that Court, be would not treat Counsel as he himself had been treated on one occasion. But he had sense enough to realize that a good many judges must have said that at the Bar and failed to appreciate that, in due course, they gave a perfect performance themselves of the conduct they had previously deplored. As the late Mr Justice Salter once remarked: 'When I was at the Bar I'm bound to say that I found some judges extraordinarily wooden-headed. I had to say the same thing over and over again to them. And, now I'm on the Bench, I can't understand why counsel are always repeating themselves.'

Roger soon found that one of the difficulties with which the Court of Criminal Appeal has to contend is the low standard of representation which often occurs, and another, the very large number of cases with which they have to deal, the vast majority of them being entirely without merit. Judges, being human, may after much experience of this, tend to expect cases to have no merit. Moreover, like the lady whom Roger had encountered at the cocktail party, they consider it just as much an injustice for a plainly guilty man to be acquitted as for a possibly innocent man to be convicted.

The Court normally consists of three judges and the procedure is for one of the three to go thoroughly into each case before the Court sits. One of the cases with which Roger had to deal arose in a rather curious way.

The Honourable Mrs X was a lady who liked beautiful clothes and gay parties, and betting on horses. She liked her husband, too, but he was not always able to keep her provided with the money which she needed to indulge her various tastes. Ladies of that kind often have accounts with one or more bookmakers and from time to time they have to ask the bookmaker to give them a little more time to pay losing bets. The bookmaker nearly always obliges, and usually gets paid in the end. He seldom has to report clients of this kind as defaulters. The point about these ladies is that there is seldom a moment when they will not find a windfall of fifty pounds extraordinarily useful. If they have no pressing commitments, the purchase of a new hat and a pair of shoes makes a morning pass very pleasantly.

A search through the list of clients of any big bookmaker will inevitably disclose the names and addresses of some ladies in this category. Mr Mowler had at one time been employed by Messrs Vulgans, who were bookmakers in a very big way. The Hon. Mrs X was one of their clients and they had paid her a considerable sum of money over the years. She had paid them considerably more. One day the Hon. Mrs X received the following letter from Mr Mowler:

Dear Madam,

I was until recently employed by Messrs Vulgans where I had charge of your account. I have now left to set up business on my own account and hope that you may care to let me have some of your investments. I can assure you of the best possible odds and of every consideration in the conduct of your account.

At that stage the Hon. Mrs X nearly threw the letter away. It was one of a pattern she knew well, and she had no desire at all to open a new account with another bookmaker. But her eye could not help noting further down in the letter the figure of £50, which was in slightly larger type than the rest of the letter. So she read on:

Whether or not you open an account with me, there is, however, a matter I feel I must mention, as it has been rather on my conscience for some time. You may remember that you backed the winner of the Oaks last June. Your actual stake was £5. By some mischance, the responsibility for which was entirely mine, I worked out the amount due to you at Starting Price odds, whereas you had in fact placed your commission at Totalisator odds. The result was that you were paid an amount which was some £50 less than the amount to which you were entitled – the actual sum due to you being £103 3s. 0d. whereas you were paid only £52 10s. 0d. I did not notice the mistake until some time afterwards and I then found, to my dismay, that I had made the same mistake with a number of clients. One or two of them complained and the matter had been adjusted, but the others, like you, had apparently not noticed the error. I need hardly say that my employers were extremely annoyed with me over the mistakes which were brought to light by the complaints, and I'm afraid that, when I discovered the other mistakes, I hadn't the courage to own up. But I did make a note of those clients who had been let down, being determined that, if ever I was able to do so, I should make it up to them. I am delighted to say that that time has now arrived. My business has prospered so well that I am now in a position to make full restitution to everyone. And I should make it plain, lest you think that this is just a catchpenny, that there are no conditions attached to my offer at all, and that, if you do not choose to become my client, I shall pay you just the same. I left my late employers in rather a hurry and unfortunately the list of names and addresses got mislaid and I was unable to find it. I am, therefore, relying on my memory but I feel reasonably certain that in your case it is accurate. If, therefore, you will be good enough to sign the form below and confirm that the money is due to you I shall be pleased to send you my cheque (or cash if you prefer it) for £50 13s. 0d. If, thereafter, you choose to become a client of this firm I shall he pleased to open a credit account immediately with a daily limit of £50 (weekly £250) and your code name will be VENDOR.

With apologies for the mistake, and in the hope of receiving your forgiveness and future commissions,

Yours sincerely,

Arthur Mowler

Below was a form:

I confirm that last June I placed with Messrs Vulgans a winning bet of £5 on the Oaks Stakes at totalisator odds and that by mistake I was paid only at starting price odds. Please send me £50 13s. 0d. in accordance with your letter.

(Signed)   Name:

Address:

Date:

PS I shall naturally be grateful if you will refrain from drawing the attention of Messrs Vulgans to this letter, and I am afraid that I cannot undertake to pay you if you do. I am sure you will understand this.

Mr Mowler prepared similar letters for despatch to a number of other ladies, who appeared to him to have the necessary qualifications. The amounts were slightly different in each case, and he did not send the other letters until he tried the effect on the Hon. Mrs X.

Now, when Mr Mowler wrote these letters he knew quite well that none of the ladies in question had made winning bets on the Oaks. They had either not backed anything at all or they had lost. He also knew that, though regular backers may easily forget whether they have or have not backed horses in all sorts of races, they will not forget having backed the winner of the Derby or the Oaks. They might forget the exact amount of their winnings or losses, but, if they have backed the winner, they will remember it very well, and will from time to time during that current racing year, and it may well be for a year or two thereafter, tell their friends that they backed it.

The average person, who backs horses, has two qualities, stupidity and greed. Stupidity, because he is going to lose in the end, greed, because he wants something for nothing. There are, of course, some kind, unselfish, and intelligent backers of horses, but there are not many, and, as Mr Mowler rightly guessed from a careful perusal of her account before he left Messrs Vulgans, the Hon. Mrs X was not one of them.

When she got the letter she realized at once that a mistake, as she thought, had been made. She knew quite well that she had not backed the winner of the Oaks. But within a quarter of an hour of the receipt of the letter she had not only convinced herself that she had backed the winner, but she actually remembered wondering why the amount she had received was so small and deciding that she must remember to query it. Within twenty minutes, she had filled in the form and within half an hour it was in the post on its way back to Mr Mowler.

The Hon. Mrs X worked it out that she ought to get a reply by the Friday. That would be very convenient for Sandown. But no reply came by the Friday or Saturday, and she was just beginning to wonder whether it was a hoax when Mr Mowler himself telephoned to know when she would be in alone. The Hon. Mrs X was delighted to make an appointment during the day, when her husband would be at the office. She had not mentioned the matter to him, as she knew him to be a man of the most ridiculous integrity, who would never have agreed to her signing the form. She knew that, though she might convince herself that she had won on the Oaks, she would never convince him. So she waited expectantly by herself for Mr Mowler, and at the appointed time two gentlemen arrived.

'Mr Mowler,' she said, holding out her hand.

'I'm afraid not, ma'am,' said one of the two – not taking the proffered hand. 'We've come to see you about him. May we come in? We're from the Criminal Investigation Department of Scotland Yard.'

The Hon. Mrs X went white for a moment, but she soon recovered herself and asked the gentlemen in and invited them to sit down.

'Yes,' she said. 'What is it you want?'

'Is this your signature, ma'am?' said the first man, bringing out the form she had signed and torn off from the bottom of Mr Mowler's letter.

'Let me see,' she said, and took the form in her hand.

The first man kept his hand on it at the same time. After a pause: 'Yes,' she said. 'I think it is.'

'Think, ma'am?' said the first man. 'Have you any doubt about it, ma'am? If you have, I must ask you to be kind enough to give me some specimens of – '

But Mrs X interrupted.

'Yes, it is my signature. What about it? Is it a fraud? Are you looking for Mr Mowler?'

'We've seen Mr Mowler, ma'am,' was the reply, 'but you'll forgive me not answering the first part of your question for the moment.'

Mrs X began to have a horrible feeling in the pit of her stomach.

'Now, ma'am,' the man went on, 'you say in that form that you had a winning bet on the Oaks with Messrs Vulgans.' He stopped.

'Yes,' answered Mrs X – when she could stand the silence no longer.

'You knew that by making that statement you would receive fifty pounds thirteen shillings?'

'I haven't had it.'

'No, ma'am, you haven't, but you hoped that by making that statement you would get it?'

'Well, what if I did?' asked Mrs X. 'That's what the letter suggested I should do, didn't it?'

'Yes, ma'am, it did – if the statement was true. Was it true, ma'am? Did you back the winner of the Oaks?'

Mrs X did not answer for a moment.

'How did you place your bets, ma'am? By telephone?'

'Yes – except on the course.'

'Did you back the winner of the Oaks by telephone then, or on the course?'

There was no answer.

'Surely, ma'am, you remember if you went to the Oaks?'

Yes, thought Mrs X, it's hopeless to lie about that. 'No – I didn't go to the Oaks.'

'Then you backed the winner by telephone?'

'I suppose so.'

'I should tell you, ma'am, that we've just come from Messrs Vulgans, where we have inspected your account.'

Mrs X said nothing, until the silence made her say – 'Well?'

'And we find, ma'am, that you did not back the winner of the Oaks.'

'Then – then – I must have made a mistake,' said Mrs X.

'A mistake which would have cost Mr Mowler fifty pounds thirteen shillings.'

She hated the way he always put in the thirteen shillings; why not just say fifty pounds? There was something so like the steam-roller of the law when he said the thirteen shillings just as deliberately as the fifty pounds.

'I'm afraid I must now warn you, ma'am, that anything you now say will be taken down in writing and may be given in evidence at your trial.'

'My trial?' exclaimed Mrs X with deep anxiety in her voice. 'What for?'

'They call it fraud, ma'am, to make an untrue statement in order to get money, ma'am.'

'But it was a mistake – I'd forgotten.'

'That's what they all say, I'm afraid, ma'am. But don't be too upset, ma'am, the jury sometimes believe them.'

'The jury? Am I going to be tried before a jury?'

'Well, you go before a magistrate first, ma'am, and then you get what's called committed for trial to the Sessions or Assizes, ma'am. But, of course, you'll be able to have solicitor and counsel to defend you, ma'am. And I shouldn't be too upset, ma'am. A lot of guilty people get off.'

'But I'm not guilty,' said Mrs X, not very convincingly.

'Then you've all the more chance, haven't you, ma'am? Now, I'm afraid we must be on our way, ma'am. We'll see ourselves out. Thank you so much, ma'am. So very sorry to have had to trouble you.'

They left and the Hon. Mrs X burst into tears. If only I'd thrown the beastly thing in the wastepaper basket. The lives of a good many people like Mrs X contain a good many 'if onlys'. Most people have their fair share of them in childhood, but the weaker sort carry on with them for most of their lives. Whether it's a kiss, a bet, an angry word, a letter, that extra glass – or a little form asking for fifty pounds thirteen shillings – if only I hadn't, if only, if only – What was she to do? She would have to tell her husband. But it would be as dreadful for him as for her. It was at a time like this that people see things in their proper perspective. She did love her husband. He wasn't just a convenience. But what was she to do? She knew she was guilty. Those policemen and lawyers would tie her up in no time. She could hear her weak little protest of 'mistake' getting fainter and fainter until it became an admission of guilt and a plea for mercy. But there would be no mercy for her – even if they didn't send her to prison, it would be in all the papers:

Appearing to feel her position acutely, the Hon. Mrs X held her face in her hands as the judge pronounced sentence.

I wish I were dead, she thought – and said.

It was just at that stage that Mr Mowler telephoned. He seemed anxious: 'Mrs X,' he said, 'have two CID officers just been round to see you?'

'Yes,' said Mrs X tearfully, 'they have.'

Mr Mowler noted that his timing was just about as perfect as he could have hoped.

'I'm terribly sorry,' he went on. 'It must have been very distressing for you.'

Hope started to rise in Mrs X. She never considered why he should be telephoning. She only knew that he sounded kind.

'I must see what I can do,' he said, and then stopped for a moment. 'Look,' he went on, 'is anyone with you? Because this is rather confidential.'

'No – there's no one.'

'Well – I'm terribly sorry about this. I am really. I never meant them to act so soon – with you, that is. I must see what I can do.' He paused, as though thinking. 'Now, let me see,' he went on. 'The trouble is that, once you start these fellows off, there's no holding them. I'd better tell you what happened. You see, I've had so many fraudulent claims made on me that I just had to turn the whole thing over to my accountants and the police. Cost me a pretty penny, I can tell you. These accountants charge the earth. But I never meant them to get on to you so quickly. I'm sure that in your case it was just a mistake.'

'Oh, it was – it was,' said Mrs X.

'I'd stake my oath on that,' said Mr Mowler. 'I know you aren't the sort of lady to do a chap down.'

'No, of course I wouldn't. I am grateful to you for seeing it like that.'

'The trouble is to stop these johnnies carrying on. They won't take any notice of me. The law's slow enough, but once you put your penny in the slot and the machine starts, it goes on and on – just like a steam-roller, and no one can stop it, not even the judges themselves.' He stopped again for a moment. 'But we've got to do something in your case. We can't have nice ladies like you dragged through the Courts. When's the prosecution starting – did he say?'

'He said something about a magistrate's court or Sessions or Assizes, but he didn't say when.'

'Humph – look, I've an idea – but you'll have to back me up.'

'Yes?'

'Suppose I tell them you did have the bet after all?'

'But they've been to Vulgans, and saw that I didn't.'

'Yes, but I could say that I took it myself and didn't book it up – hoping it would lose or something like that. They're bound to believe me, as I've nothing to gain.'

'Would you really say that for me?'

'Well – as I see it, it's the only way. It's a bit of risk for me, of course, but – ' he paused again. Then: 'I tell you what – you help me and I'll help you.'

'What can I do?'

'Well, I told you about my accountant's charges, they're too dreadful for words. It's almost better to pay the tax. Costs you more to get advice how to avoid it. But you don't want to hear my troubles. Now – look – I can see a way out for both of us. You give me a hand with my accountant's charges, and I'll tell the police I've made a mistake. Then you needn't feel it's all on one side.'

'How much?' asked Mrs X cautiously.

'Well, it's up to you, isn't it? I don't expect anything. Certainly not more than, say, ten per cent of what I've got to pay. Yes – how about that? – you let me have fifty guineas.'

'Fifty guineas!' said Mrs X.

'Look,' said Mr Mowler, 'I think we'd better wash the whole thing out. You obviously think I'm trying to sting you, when I was only trying to help. No – we'll just let things take their course. I can manage all right.'

'No – please, Mr Mowler,' said Mrs X, very anxiously indeed. 'I'd like to help – really I would.'

'That's very nice of you, I'm sure,' said Mr Mowler. 'But you only say that because you're excited. No, I don't really see why I should risk getting into trouble with the police just because you've got a nice voice on the telephone. No, Mrs X, I think we'll leave things as they are,' and Mr Mowler rang off.

After a few frantic attempts to re-engage him, Mrs X started to walk sadly away from the telephone. A few seconds later it rang again.

'Is that Hammersmith 7835?' said Mr Mowler.

'No,' said Mrs X. 'This is Mrs X. Isn't that Mr Mowler?'

'Well,' conceded Mr Mowler grudgingly, 'it is. But we'd finished our conversation. I was trying to get another number. We must have been still connected. Goodbye again.'

'Don't ring off, Mr Mowler, please,' said Mrs X, desperately.

'Why not?' said Mr Mowler. 'What is there to say?'

'I'd like to help,' said Mrs X. 'Really I would.'

'How can I know it's true?' said Mr Mowler. 'After all, you did sign the form, didn't you? I'm afraid I'm disappointed in you Mrs X, very disappointed. I was sorry to begin with, but now I think I was wrong to be.'

'No, really – really – really, I promise,' said Mrs X. 'Where can I give you the money? Please let me, I do mean it.'

'Well, look,' said Mr Mowler. 'You mustn't blame me if I don't altogether trust you, but you do sound genuine at the moment. Now, I tell you what. You go straight to your bank and get out – how much did you say you wanted to give me?'

'Seventy pounds,' said Mrs X.

'All right,' said Mr Mowler, 'that's a fair deal. Take an envelope with you to the bank and get seventy one-pound notes. Put them in the envelope. Turn to the right when you come out of the bank and, when you've taken twelve paces, drop the envelope. I shall pick it up and give it to you, and you can give it me back again. Now, where is the bank?'

Mrs X told him.

'All right – in half an hour.'

'Wouldn't tomorrow do?' asked Mrs X.

'Of course,' said Mr Mowler, 'any time. Next week – next month – next year, but I thought you wanted me to get on to the police today.'

'I'll come at once,' said Mrs X.

Mrs X's bank manager required a little persuasion to let her have the seventy pounds in view of the state of her account, but he did so in the end, and within a very few minutes the money was in the safe keeping of Mr Mowler.

'You'll let me know about the police, won't you?' she whispered, as she gave him the envelope.

Mr Mowler winked.

'Trust me,' he said.

Nothing happened for a few days, and then Mr Mowler telephoned.

'Look,' he said, 'I've run into a snag. It's my fault. Trying to be too clever.'

'Oh – what is it?' said Mrs X anxiously.

'Well, I went to one of the CID officers you saw and said what you and I agreed, but he didn't seem to think much of it. Then, very stupidly – I can't think what made me do it – I slipped a couple of fivers into his hand. Now I'm probably going to be charged with bribery. I'm seeing my solicitor and counsel this afternoon.'

'But what about my case?' asked Mrs X.

'Coming up in a fortnight, I think they said.'

'But can't you stop it? They must believe you.'

'There's no must about it,' said Mr Mowler. 'And I'm afraid I've too many worries of my own now to worry about yours. D'you know my solicitor wants eighty pounds on account. I can't think about other people's affairs while I've got my own.'

'Look, Mr Mowler, I'll let you have eighty pounds if you'll go on helping me.'

'All right,' said Mr Mowler, 'I'll try. Meet me at the bank as before. Half an hour.'

'I shall have to borrow the money,' said Mrs X.

'Come off it,' said Mr Mowler. 'A lady like you.'

'It's quite true,' said Mrs X. 'The bank won't let me have any more.'

'All right,' said Mr Mowler. 'The same drill. Where do we meet?'

'I'll have to think,' said Mrs X. 'Can I ring you?'

'I'll ring you in ten minutes,' said Mr Mowler, 'and I'm afraid I shan't be able to wait after that.'

He rang off and Mrs X hurriedly considered whether she should pawn some jewellery or beg from a friend.

It was only after she had adopted both expedients several times, and paid Mr Mowler three hundred and fifty pounds, that it suddenly dawned on her that Mr Mowler might be leading her up the garden. There had been no further signs from the police – if they were police – she had never seen their warrant cards – no mention in the papers of any bribery case, and, once the thought occurred to her, it developed as swiftly as her belief that she had backed the winner of the Oaks. She went straight to her husband with the necessary tears.

'You blithering idiot,' he said consolingly, and went to the police.

The next time Mr Mowler picked up the little envelope and handed it to Mrs X, and received it back again, he had not gone more than a few paces when he felt a hand on his shoulder.

'We're police officers. What is in that envelope?'

'Hell,' said Mr Mowler, 'I might have known it was too good to be true. If only I'd stopped before.'

They arrested Mr Mowler, but they could not find his two confederates who had pretended to be CID officers. Mr Mowler expressed complete ignorance of their existence.

'You've only Mrs X's word for their existence, and she isn't too particular what she says,' he said.

'She didn't invent *them*,' said the inspector, who was in charge of the matter.

'Well, perhaps it *was* two of your chaps,' volunteered Mr Mowler hopefully. 'After all, she had committed a crime attempting to obtain money by false pretences. You ought to have been after her even if you weren't.'

'Come on, Mowler, you're for it anyway,' said the inspector, 'If you'll help us land your pals we'll put in a good word for you when the matter of sentence arises.'

'Not a very tactful approach, inspector,' said Mr Mowler. 'Even if they were my pals – which they were not – d'you think I'd give them away to save my own skin? Not on your life. Haven't sunk as low as that.'

'And how low d'you call blackmail?' asked the inspector.

'Blackmail!' said Mr Mowler – 'you can't charge me with blackmail. Where are the threats?'

'If our lawyers can't make what you've been doing into blackmail I'll agree for once that the law's an ass,' said the inspector.

'Well – how are they going to do it? I haven't made any threats. Nor did anyone else. Even my pals, as you call them, they only asked questions. Very sensible ones, too, if I may say so.'

But when they brought Mr Mowler to trial, in addition to charges of fraud there were three charges of blackmail against him, namely that he and certain persons unknown demanded with menaces and with intent to steal seventy pounds, eighty pounds, and two hundred pounds from Mrs X contrary to Section 30 of the Larceny Act, 1916.

'Who thought that one out?' said Mr Mowler. 'Anyway, I'd nothing to do with the other chaps. So you can't bring in what they said. It isn't evidence.'

But the judge at the trial ruled otherwise and it was pointed out that, if Mr Mowler knew nothing about the supposed CID officers, it was odd that, when he telephoned Mrs X, just after they had left, he had asked whether they had called on her. When Mr Mowler saw the significance of this, he promptly denied that he had been the first to mention the CID officers. He said that Mrs X had mentioned them first, and added: 'Why believe her rather than me? We know she's prepared to tell a lie – if it's made worth her while.'

In fact Mr Mowler defended himself with great perseverance and ability. And he hadn't the embarrassment, which some barrister defending him might have had, of believing the client to be guilty. He knew he was, and was not in the least embarrassed in denying it.

'Members of the jury,' he said in his final address, 'you will, I hope, overlook any deficiencies in my address to you. I have not the training and experience of my learned friend.'

'Don't call counsel your "learned friend",' said the judge.

'Now I've forgotten what I was going to say,' said Mr Mowler – quick to try to obtain the sympathy of the lay jury for the layman. 'You see, members of the jury, I've made a mistake already. It's very difficult for an ignorant, inexperienced person, unlearned in the ways of the law, to compete with the expert. But I must do my best – or it will go hard with my client. Is that all right, my Lord?'

'You won't find that trying to he funny or impertinent will do you any good with the jury,' said the judge. 'You've chosen to defend yourself. You could have had counsel allotted to you, if you'd wanted.'

'But think what counsel, my Lord. Would you care to be defended by one of them, my Lord?'

'Don't be insolent,' said the Judge, 'and continue with your address.'

Mr Mowler looked for sympathy to the jury.

'I'm sorry, my Lord,' he said. 'I'm sorry, members of the jury – I'm doing my best. It isn't easy – when you're fighting for your life – for that's what it is. You've never been in prison, members of the jury, but wouldn't you prefer death to fifteen years' imprisonment – and that's the penalty for the crimes I'm charged with.'

'That's the *maximum* penalty,' said the judge.

'There I am again,' said Mr Mowler. 'Always putting my foot in it. But, if you convict me, members of the jury, d'you think his Lordship's attitude suggests anything less than the maximum? Did he interrupt counsel's speech like he interrupts me?'

'Counsel did not make false or unfair assertions, nor was he alternately insolent and impertinent. If he had been, he would have been treated the same way.'

'To resume, members of the jury,' continued Mr Mowler, as it were, wearily, 'I was saying, when I caused his Lordship displeasure for the I don't-know-how-manyeth-time – I was saying – now I've forgotten again.'

'If you dealt with the facts, instead of keeping off them and making stupid or impertinent remarks, you might do better,' said the judge.

'Perhaps you'd make my speech for me, my Lord,' said Mr Mowler – who knew that, as soon as he came to deal with the facts, he was in difficulties, but who hoped that, by baiting the judge, he might get sufficient sympathy from the jury to procure his acquittal on the more serious charge.

'Does that mean you've finished?' asked the judge.

Mr Mowler made a mute appeal with his head and eyes to the jury, and then said: 'Is that what your Lordship really thinks?'

'How dare you speak to me like that!' said the judge. 'When this case is over I may deal with you for contempt of court.'

'That makes it all the easier for me to address the jury,' said Mr Mowler, 'doesn't it? "Never mind what they do. I'll put you inside in due course." Why bother about a trial! I thought this was a court of justice. Have they taken the figure down from up top? If they haven't, they ought to.'

'Now, look,' said the judge, 'I don't want to have to do this, but I must, if you force me. If you persist in being rude, instead of addressing the jury about the facts of the case, I shall postpone this case until next sessions and discharge this jury from giving a verdict.'

'Will *you* be here, then?' asked Mr Mowler.

The judge had now to carry out his threat or, in effect, admit defeat and give Mr Mowler free rein.

'Very well,' said the judge, 'I'm extremely sorry, members of the jury, that your time has been wasted, but it is impossible for a trial to be properly conducted like this.'

'Who's fault's that?' put in Mr Mowler.

'Take the prisoner below,' said the judge, and went on to discharge the jury in his absence.

At the next sessions, Mr Mowler was not so fortunate, for the presiding judge was Mr Justice Hathaway. Mr Mowler had rightly judged that his only chance in all the circumstances was to get the judge at loggerheads with the jury, and the only way to do that was to goad him into being unfair or at any rate giving an appearance of unfairness. It is fairly easy for the prisoner in person to obtain sympathy, if he goes the right way about it. There is the poor little man, with the whole of the law ranged against him, and, if the judge is against him too, there is only the jury left. It may well be that Mr Mowler had overdone it, and had not succeeded in his efforts. But, however that may be, it was a hopeless task to do the same with Mr Justice Hathaway, who responded to every attempt by Mr Mowler to provoke him, with a kindly remark – which made the judge the object of sympathy rather than the prisoner. However, Mr Mowler was nothing if not persistent, and he had another card to play. He knew that sympathy is always against a blackmailer. He started his speech to the jury like this: 'Members of the jury,' he said, 'I'm not sure that I'm really in a condition to address you properly. I've been in prison an extra two months for nothing – unconvicted, unsentenced – just because the other judge didn't like me to address the jury in my own way. It isn't justice to interrupt a prisoner when he's addressing the jury, but he did it all the time, and when he found the jury were taking some notice and would probably have acquitted me, he sent me to the cells and told the jury to go home. Why should I be tried twice? Is it fair?'

Mr Justice Hathaway said nothing. So Mr Mowler turned directly to him: 'Is it fair, my Lord?'

Mr Justice Hathaway still said nothing.

'I'm speaking to you, my Lord,' said Mr Mowler. 'I know I'm only the prisoner, but haven't I the right to have the assistance of the court?'

'Of course,' said the judge. 'I'm so sorry. I thought it was a rhetorical question.'

'I don't understand long words, my Lord, I'm not educated like your Lordship and my learned friends of the Bar.'

'That's all right,' said the judge. 'You're doing very well. I wish everyone were as well defended.'

'I'm not doing well at all, and you know it,' said Mr Mowler.

'Mr Mowler,' said the judge, 'I'm sure we understand one another. I think yours is one of the most brilliant efforts I have ever seen. You ought to have gone to the Bar.'

Mr Mowler looked wearily at the jury.

'I don't know which is worse,' he said, 'threats or sarcasm.'

'I assure you there was no sarcasm intended,' said the judge. 'If I gave you a different impression, I apologize. Yours is one of the most brilliant performances I have seen. If you deal with the facts as well as you have dealt with what I may call preliminary matters, you should make a profound impression on the jury, and, I may say, on me.'

Mr Mowler realized that he was fighting a losing battle. No one could get angry with Mr Justice Hathaway, and to be rude to him was like hitting a child. As a last resort, but without much hope, he tried slightly different tactics.

'His Lordship', he said, 'is as kind and good a judge as I could wish to appear before, but, members of the jury, you musn't be deceived by the gentle glance and the kindly word. It's his Lordship's duty to get me convicted if he possibly can, and his method is – until I'm convicted – to use the velvet glove. You'd think butter wouldn't melt in his mouth. But just wait till you've found me guilty. Then you'll see. He'll send me down for the count, I tell you – imprisonment for life, that's what I'm up against, and don't you forget it. Now you may think, members of the jury, that though I don't pretend that what I've done was right, Mrs X got no more than she deserved. She, with all her money – all her education – all her chances – was quite prepared to tell a lie to get money out of someone whom she wouldn't smile at across the street. Oh – I know all about the Welfare State and no class distinctions, but you've seen the lady in the witness box – you know the type. At least I hope you do. Well – did she get more than she deserved? I didn't go for some poor little defenceless country girl. I shouldn't expect any sympathy if I had. I went for someone who'd no business to be tempted. But she fell for it, like a kitten after a reel of cotton. If anyone ought to be in the dock, it's she. She tried to obtain money by false pretences all right. That's one thing there's no doubt about. Isn't such a person what you might call fair game? I'm no Robin Hood. I don't pretend I was going to give the money to hospitals, and all that. But if ever a person ought to have been shown up for what she was, it's

Mrs X. What right has she to hold her head high in society, when she told a lie to get fifty pounds. But *she's* allowed to be called Mrs X. Is that fair? Why should I get all the stick? Well now, you may say, "That's all very well, what can we do about it? We don't like Mrs X, but the prisoner did have the money off her, and he did tell her a lot of taradiddles to get it." All right, members of the jury, I did, and I'm not saying you couldn't convict me of obtaining by false pretences. Mind you, I'd prefer you not to, but I'm not saying you can't. But it's this other charge I'm really fighting. And the only bit of evidence against me is that I'm supposed to have spoken about the CID to her first. Well, I say I didn't. And why shouldn't you believe me rather than her? And, if there's a doubt in your mind, I'm entitled to it. So that's what I ask you to do. Wash out the blackmail charge, and, if you convict me on the other, you can always recommend me to mercy, if you think fit. And I suggest that a couple of looks at Mrs X should make you want to think fit. That's all, members of the jury, thank you for being so patient – and your Lordship.'

But in spite of his struggles, the jury convicted Mr Mowler on all counts, and Mr Justice Hathaway sentenced him apologetically to a total of twelve years' imprisonment. It was from that sentence that he appealed to the Court of Criminal Appeal, and it fell to Roger, in the first instance, to consider the appeal. After he had read the transcript of the evidence at the trial, he went to Mr Justice Breeze, who was to be one of the other judges.

'I'm only a new boy,' said Roger, 'but it seems rather a lot to me. He's only been to prison once before.'

'Blackmail is always expensive,' said Breeze.

'I realize that, of course,' said Roger, 'and it's a bad case. Similar letters to several other ladies were found at his address, and no doubt they'd have received his attention in due course. But the maximum for each offence was only five years.'

'Apart from that are there any redeeming features?'

'Only his age – thirty-eight – if that can be called a redeeming feature, and the fact that he's only been to prison once before.'

'For false pretences, I suppose?'

'Yes, he got six months.'

'Humph. He's gone up in the weights. Six months to twelve years. All the same Hathaway's a pretty good handicapper.'

'I don't understand the language,' said Roger, 'but I suppose the metaphor is something to do with horses.'

'You're coming on, Roger. Tell me, have you ever had any vices? Your wife must find you a very dull fellow.'

'I break out and go to the cinema occasionally,' said Roger.

' "U" certificate, I suppose?'

'Of course, unless I have an adult with me. But what d'you think of this? Mrs X certainly deserved what she got, I suppose, but then they're the only people that can be blackmailed.'

'How true. Chaps like you are unassailable, unless, of course, you're framed in some way – snapped with a girl on your knee – or something.'

'What did you say!' said Roger.

'Unless you're framed, I said. You haven't been, I suppose? But no one would want to. It's extraordinary that no criminals or litigants, however bad or mad, try to get their own back on the judges they've appeared before.'

'It's a pretty good compliment, I suppose, to our impartiality.'

'You won't let it make you pompous, I hope,' said Breeze. 'That's a failing some of us have suffered from.'

'Not you, anyway.'

'Thank you. No, I have some other failings. Breeze by name and breeze by nature, they say. Well, it's true, I suppose. And I must say I don't give a fig for what people say. You'd be horrified at the things I do. The other day I went to Brighton races. Did you see the picture in the *Daily Journal*? I was in the paddock. "Is he as good a judge of horseflesh as he is of people?" Well, I could have given them the answer on that occasion. No, decidedly no. I backed three losers.'

'Do you often go racing?' asked Roger.

'Once or twice a year. Why not? Helps me to understand my fellow men better. Now, when I get a case about trainers and jockeys, I know what they're talking about. You'd have to start from scratch.'

'Well – I have been on a racecourse,' said Roger.

'Dear, dear,' said Breeze. 'Disguised, I suppose?'

'Oh, I didn't mean since I was appointed,' said Roger.

'Oh, well,' said Breeze, 'so long as you're happy, it doesn't matter. Have you always been so solemn, or are you weighed down by the responsibilities of your appointment?'

'No,' said Roger, 'it's not that. I've always been like this really. Fortunately my wife doesn't seem to mind.'

Breeze thought for a moment.

'Women are wonderful,' he said. 'How have I managed to do without one?'

'There's still time,' said Roger. 'But what about Mrs X?'

'No, I don't think I should care for her.'

'But what about the twelve years?' persisted Roger. 'Is it all right, d'you think?'

'Sorry, I was thinking about something else. Twelve years is a lot. I'm not sure. I see he pleaded not guilty, and fought all the way. Has he helped the police at all?'

'No. Won't give the names of his friends.'

'Well, I must say that's the only good thing you've said about him so far. Blackmailers usually haven't many redeeming features, but that's certainly one. You can be quite sure they've asked him often enough.'

'Of course,' said Roger, 'it was his case that they were nothing to do with him. So he couldn't very well give their names and addresses.'

'Yes, I see. Well, from what you tell me it's a really bad case. Carefully thought out. The victim threatened by bogus policemen, and squeezed and squeezed unmercifully. And other victims all ready to be dealt with. I'll think about it.'

In due course the application for leave to appeal came on for hearing and Mr Mowler was allowed to appear before the Court and speak on his own behalf. He found the three judges in scarlet more awe-inspiring than he had expected. While in prison he had spoken airily of the way he was going to speak to them, if they did not look like reducing his sentence.

'They can't do any more to you,' he said to an old hand. 'Might as well get something for your money.'

'They can add a bit.'

'What, to twelve years?'

'My boy,' said the old hand, 'when you've been in this business as long as I have, you'll know that there's nothing they can't do. You take my advice and speak oily. It pays.'

'What, with them?'

'I once had three years knocked off. But I wouldn't have, if I'd gone about it your way. Now, you'd have attacked the judge I was appealing from. A perishing so-and-so you'd have called him. And so he was. I called him that too, and some more, but to myself. When I was up before them redskins I said I wouldn't have wanted to be tried by a better or finer judge but I did feel that though I deserved the sentence, if they took a bit off, it'd help me to go straight when I came out, really it would. I was getting on in years and ten years was an awful long time at my age. So they made it seven. So don't forget, when you're up there. Make it oily.'

And, in the circumstances, Mr Mowler found it easier to take the advice he had beer given than he would have found it to behave as he had behaved at his trial.

'My Lords,' he said towards the end of his address, 'would it make any difference if I give the names of the men who were in with me?'

Breeze whispered to Roger.

'I was going to suggest knocking something off until he said that. I told you blackmailers had no redeeming qualities.'

He looked at Mr Mowler.

'It is always open to you to help the police if you choose to do so and the Home Secretary can, if he wishes, consider whether such help as you may give justifies remission of sentence. As far as this Court is concerned, we do not make bargains with appellants. If you'd wanted to help the police you could have done so long ago. Is there anything else you want to say?'

'Twelve years is a terrible long time,' said Mr Mowler.

'Blackmail', replied the judge, 'is nearly always a very serious crime but sometimes the blackmailer has drifted or been tempted to blackmail. In your case, it was a carefully and ingeniously prepared plot. You deliberately set out to procure someone to commit a crime in order that you might batten on her and, if you had not been caught, it is plain that the other persons whose names and addresses were found at your home would have received the letters you had already prepared. Did you ever consider the effect on Mrs X or her family of your extortion? Some people are driven to suicide by people like you.'

'She shouldn't have signed the form, my Lord, then nothing would have happened to her.'

'You shouldn't have sent it to her,' said Roger. 'Then nothing would have happened to you.'

And the appeal was dismissed.

'Make it oily!' said Mr Mowler, as they took him down to the cells. 'I wish I could have made it boiling oily.'

CHAPTER FOURTEEN

Oranges

'I'm glad you didn't reduce that sentence,' said Anne.

'You sound as though you might have been caught by him,' said Roger.

'Well, out of consideration for you, I shouldn't have been. But there are an awful lot of silly women around, who'd sign anything almost for fifty pounds.'

'But isn't that the only point in his favour?' said Roger. 'He'd only catch worthless people.'

'I wouldn't say worthless,' said Anne. 'There are a lot of otherwise quite decent people who smuggle things through the customs.'

'I'm glad you said "otherwise",' said Roger. 'I dislike that sort of thing.'

'What are you doing tomorrow?'

'I'm sitting in a Divisional Court with old Breeze.'

'I see he gave that girl a hundred and fifty pounds.'

'Yes,' said Roger. 'Plummer did pretty well out of that.'

'Did you expect him to give more?'

'No, it wasn't that,' said Roger, 'but his club got terrific advertisement out of it. Pretty well worth it.'

'He hasn't been badgering you recently. D'you think he's been trying someone else?'

'I hope so,' said Roger. 'I've had my fair share. Oh, by the way,' he added, 'I won't be in to dinner tomorrow. Harrison is up for the night and wants me to dine with him.'

'Harrison? I thought for the moment that you were going to say that you were dining with Toni.'

Roger blushed.

'Why on earth should you think that?' he said.

'No idea,' said Anne. 'Silly of me.'

But she would have felt, at the least, a little worried if she had heard Toni tell Plummer that morning that she was dining with her judge that night.

Next day, when Roger and Breeze entered their Court, Plummer was sitting three rows behind counsel. He bowed slightly as they sat down.

'I know that face,' whispered Breeze to Roger.

'Don't take any notice of him,' said Roger, and explained Plummer's little habits in Court.

The case before them arose out of an arbitration.

'There used to be a man who stood outside the Law Courts,' said Breeze, shortly after the case had begun, 'who carried a board with "arbitrate, don't litigate," on it. He was a friend to the lawyers, if ever there was one. This case is a good example. It took seven days before the arbitrator. Counsel were employed on both sides. It came to the High Court, up to the Court of Appeal, back to the arbitrator for another three days. And now here we have it again. If it had been an ordinary case brought in the ordinary way it wouldn't have cost half the money. Litigation's bad enough, but arbitration's ten times worse.'

'Except, perhaps, my Lord,' put in counsel, 'for real trade arbitrations.'

'You mean,' said Breeze, 'when an expert just looks at the goods and says these are up to sample or they're not. Yes, I agree, that's better than all of us put together. But it's the only kind of arbitration that is. Well, we'd better get on, I suppose.'

Counsel continued his speech. Every now and then Roger and Breeze interrupted with a comment or a question. To which counsel would often reply: 'With respect, no, my Lord,' or 'With respect, my Lord, I would say etc. etc.'

Eventually Breeze said: 'By "with respect", Mr Cling, you mean, don't you, "surely you're not serious when you say that"?'

' "With respect" is shorter, my Lord,' said counsel.

'A good point,' said Breeze. 'Pity you haven't a few more like that. As far as I can see, your client, who contracted to supply oranges, supplied orange juice. Why isn't he liable in damages?'

'The terms of the contract, my Lord.'

'The contract said oranges.'

'It said a good deal more than that, my Lord – with respect.'

Breeze laughed.

'I wish your client had your merits, Mr Cling,' he said. He turned to Roger and whispered: 'I like this chap. D'you know him?'

'A bit,' said Roger. 'He's good, don't you think?'

'He won't let me blow him out of Court, if that's what you mean. Yes, Mr Cling, you were explaining how the law of this country permits a man who contracts to deliver oranges to deliver orange juice instead, and get away with it.'

'It wasn't all orange juice, my Lord. There were some oranges.'

'Only about a tenth of the total quantity. If you came back from the greengrocer with one orange out of ten, what d'you think your wife would say to you if you explained that the other nine had leaked through the bag?'

'Fortunately, my Lord,' said Mr Cling, 'or unfortunately, I am not in your Lordship's happy position, and it couldn't happen to me.'

'Well, if you had a wife, what d'you suppose she'd say? She'd send you back for the other nine, wouldn't she?'

'But in that case, my Lord, there would have been no special contract between me and the greengrocer.'

'Special contract!' said Breeze. 'They bought oranges. You might just as well say that a contract to deliver butter can be fulfilled by the delivery of soap.'

'With respect, no, my Lord. If your Lordship said milk and cheese, that would be a closer analogy.'

'All right, Mr Cling, I'll accept your suggestion. A contract to supply milk. The milk has turned to cheese on delivery. Cannot the buyer complain?'

'No doubt he will complain, my Lord, but whether successfully or not will depend upon the terms of the contract.'

'Well, if I buy milk, I expect milk, not cheese, and if I buy oranges, I expect oranges, not orange juice.' He leaned towards Roger.

'Wake up,' he said. 'What d'you think? Don't leave it all to me.'

'I think it depends on the terms of the contract,' said Roger.

'You ruddy lawyers, you're all the same,' whispered Breeze.

'My brother seems to think cheese will do,' said Breeze. 'We'd better hear what your opponent has to say.'

Meanwhile Plummer, finding that his approbation or disapprobation was having no observable effect, wrote a note on a piece of paper and asked the usher to give it to

Roger. 'Toni will be coming into Court any moment,' it read. Roger screwed up the piece of paper, put it in the pocket of his gown and tried not to look in Plummer's direction. Half an hour later Breeze was just saying to Mr Cling's opponent: 'Apparently your client was unwise enough – unwise enough – ' he stopped.

He had suddenly noticed Toni come into Court. 'Unwise enough,' he went on, 'to make a contract under which he had to take the oranges even if they arrived as orange juice.'

'Contracts must be read reasonably, my Lord.'

'Would you repeat that, please,' said Breeze.

Counsel obliged.

'Are you saying that my brother Thursby is reading it unreasonably?'

'With respect, yes, my Lord.'

Breeze again leaned towards Roger.

'Well, stand up for yourself,' he said.

'The contract,' said Roger, 'makes express provision for oranges going bad. It makes a special allowance. That your clients have had.'

'But no one expected the consignment to go as bad as this one.'

'I dare say,' said Roger, 'but as they have provided for the contingency of oranges going bad, I don't see how your clients can get any more relief than is expressly provided for by the contract. *Expressum facit cessare tacitum.*'

'Do talk English,' whispered Breeze.

'Where express words are used there is no room for implication,' said Roger.

Breeze laughed.

'I didn't mean it,' he whispered, 'but you did it very nicely. Well, I think that will do for the day,' he added aloud, and both judges rose and left the Court.

'Well, I suppose you're right about the oranges,' he said to Roger, as they walked along the judges' corridor together. 'But, by Jove, she's a pretty girl.'

CHAPTER FIFTEEN

The Truth

Although Anne would have trusted Roger completely even if he had not been a judge, she would have been horrified to hear Toni confide to Plummer on the morning after Roger's dinner with Harrison that she was doing very nicely with her judge.

'Did he give you a good dinner?' asked Plummer.

'Lovely,' said Toni, 'and he took me somewhere where no one would be likely to recognize us.'

'Wise man,' said Plummer. 'But, you know, I don't want things carried too far.'

'But I'm enjoying myself,' protested Toni. 'I like my judge. He's so human.'

'That's what I meant,' said Plummer. 'I'd like to wipe some of the superiority off his face, but I don't want any real trouble. And his wife is charming.'

'Yes,' said Toni, 'she is nice. But it's all very well for you to blow hot and cold. One doesn't get a judge on one's hands every day.'

'Well,' said Plummer, 'if he comes a cropper, it'll be his own fault, I suppose. He shouldn't have taken on the job unless he was prepared to abide by the rules.'

Meanwhile Roger was concerned with a very different problem. It was in Court. When he was at the Bar he had been used to many kinds of witnesses, but he knew that there is in fact no limit to their variety. As a judge he was prepared for any kind, but on this occasion, a man, who was called to give evidence, gave him rather more trouble than usual and made him think more than he had done before about the whole question of witnesses and giving evidence.

There was nothing particularly interesting about the case itself. It was a claim for damages for breach of contract. The contract had been made by word of mouth only and there was a dispute between the parties as to what exactly was said when it was made. To support the defendant's version of the interview, his counsel, Mr Steaming, called a man named Jones. Mr Jones went into the witness box.

'What is your full name?' asked the associate.

'Andrew Penitent Jones.'

'Take the book in your right hand and repeat after me,' said the associate. 'I swear by Almighty God.'

Without touching the Bible Mr Jones said: 'I will do my best to tell the truth.'

'No,' said the associate, 'you must repeat the words I say, and kindly take the Bible in your right hand.'

Roger tapped his desk with a pencil and the associate turned away from the witness to speak to the judge.

'Perhaps he wants to affirm,' whispered Roger.

'Very good, my Lord,' said the associate, and then spoke to the witness again.

'If you have no religious belief, you may affirm instead of taking the oath,' he said.

'I have a deep religious belief,' said Mr Jones. 'I am a practising member of the Church of England.'

'Very well then, sir,' said the associate, 'will you kindly take the Bible in your right hand and repeat the words of the oath after me.'

'I'm afraid not,' said Mr Jones, 'but I will do my best to tell the truth.'

'Mr Jones,' intervened Roger, 'I'm afraid you must take the oath. What is your objection to doing so?'

'Well, my Lord, first of all the Bible tells us not to swear by anything. Secondly, it's much too difficult. If I did take an oath to tell the truth, I couldn't possibly break it.'

'No one wants you to,' said Roger.

'I dare say they don't, my Lord,' said Mr Jones, 'but what is the truth? I may think something to be the truth but I may be wrong.'

'Obviously,' said Roger, 'you can only do your best. I assure you that you'll come to no harm if you do your honest best to tell the truth.'

'But, my Lord,' said Mr Jones, 'your Lordship is no doubt very important, but you are not God. I may not come to any harm here, but can you speak for elsewhere?'

'Mr Jones,' said Roger, 'I appreciate your scruples and, if you give your evidence as carefully as you have considered the words of the oath, you will no doubt be an excellent witness, but in a civilized country one has to have forms and they must be complied with. If there were a different form of oath for every person the administration of justice would be impossible.'

'I don't see why, my Lord. You could provide penalties for telling deliberate lies. Then it wouldn't matter what words the witness said.'

'I'm sorry,' said Roger, 'but, while I sympathize with your point of view, I can't take up much more time arguing with you. I'm afraid I must ask you to take the oath.'

'If I agree to swear, my Lord, may I add the words: "to the best of my ability"?'

'I'm afraid not,' said Roger.

'But how can I possibly swear by God that what I am about to say is the truth, the whole truth and nothing but the truth, when I know very well I may be mistaken?'

'Nothing in the world is certain, Mr Jones,' said Roger. 'You can only swear what you believe to be the truth. That is what the oath means.'

'That isn't what it says, my Lord,' said Mr Jones. 'May I put that in – and say: "I'll swear to tell what I believe to be the truth"?'

'No,' said Roger, 'you must take the oath or affirm in the ordinary form.'

'Why should I, my Lord?' protested Mr Jones. 'It's against my conscience to do so. It's really against my conscience to swear at all, but, if I can arrange things with my conscience on that matter, I should have thought you could have arranged things on the other. It's not much I'm asking, my Lord. I only want to say what you say the oath means.'

'I'm sorry,' said Roger. 'You may affirm if you wish. But this is a Court of Law and in a Court of Law the law's forms must be observed.'

'But if you bring the Almighty into a Court of Law, my Lord, hasn't He any say in the matter? All the judges in the world can't speak for Him.'

'Now, Mr Jones,' said Roger. 'I've listened to you most patiently, but I must now ask you to take the oath.'

'In its ordinary form, my Lord?'

'Yes.'

'May I add something under my breath?'

'No.'

'May I make a mental reservation?'

'Yes, you may do that.'

'Well, really, my Lord,' said Mr Jones, 'it seems that the law isn't interested in the religious side of it at all, although it brings it in to frighten people. Apparently you wouldn't mind if I took the oath – like children tell stories – with my fingers crossed, so long as I say the words.'

'I'm afraid I can't allow you any further latitude,' said Roger. 'Will you kindly take the oath or affirm.'

'And if I refuse?'

'Then I'm afraid I shall have to commit you to prison.'

'For how long?'

'Until you have purged your contempt.'

'How could I do that, my Lord, without taking the oath or affirming?'

'I'm not sure that you could.'

'Then I might be in prison for life just because I wanted to add the only words to the oath which would make it an honest thing for me to say.'

'We'll deal with that problem if it arises,' said Roger. 'I hope it won't.' He looked at the clock. 'Mr Steaming,' he said, after a moment's thought. 'I shall rise now for the luncheon adjournment, and I can only hope that during the interval the witness will reconsider the position.'

During the adjournment Roger decided to consult one of the older judges. He realized that Mr Jones might very well insist on being sent to prison and, if possible, he wanted to avoid that situation, which could do no good to anyone and indeed might delay and prejudice the fair trial of the action. The only judge available was the oldest Queen's Bench judge, Mr Justice Pantin. He had been a judge for over thirty years at the time Roger consulted him and he was in his eighty-eighth year.

From time to time journalists had suggested that he should retire but he took no notice of their suggestions, and it was fairly plain that, unless Parliament imposed a retiring age for High Court judges, he would go on until he died. Fortunately he was in full possession of his faculties and tried his cases well. He had, however, in his later years tended to become verbose, and, though he still did justice, he was inclined to take a long time about it. In ordinary conversation he was rather worse and would sometimes take a prodigious time to come to the point. On the way to the point he would find so many interesting side-roads to go down that, unless reminded by someone who knew him well, he would sometimes forget what he was leading up to.

'Ah,' he would say, 'that reminds me of a case I once heard before Chief Justice Manners. It was a most interesting affair – unique, I should say. He was a great judge, you know. I'm not saying that his appointment was popular. It wasn't. Too much politics about it. But he proved them wrong and pretty quickly too. I was at the Bar with him, you know, and a nicer opponent you couldn't have. But a fighter, if ever there was one. You had to be awake the whole time. He rather reminded me of Coles – as an advocate, I mean. He had a deeper voice, though. But a most imposing presence. When he defied a jury to convict his client, they must really have felt they'd get into serious trouble if they did. Now, where was I?' He would then be gently reminded that he was about to tell his listener of a case which Manners CJ had tried, and off he would start again, but it was quite an event if the case was reached within a quarter of an hour.

In spite of this reputation, Roger felt that his great experience in dealing with witnesses might be of help, and he took the risk – a considerable one – of missing his lunch altogether.

'Well, my boy, what can I do for you?' he said, as Roger came into his room. Roger told him his problem. 'Ah, my boy,' said the old judge, 'a good many of us don't think enough about witnesses. I didn't at first. You've never been in the witness box, I suppose?'

Roger confessed that he had not.

'Well, of course it wouldn't be much of an ordeal for us, though, if some of us talked as much in the box as we do on the Bench, we certainly ought to get into trouble. Well, I have given evidence. A good many years ago. I can't say that I was nervous, but then I'd been at the Bar for years then. I knew the form. I wasn't in a strange place. How many of us think of the fluttering little heart in the breast of some witnesses? He looks all right, he stands up all right, his colour's all right. So we assume he is all right. Have you ever considered the self-control that might be necessary to produce that effect?'

'I can't say that I have,' said Roger.

'Well, you should, my boy. The case may be vital to the man. Just think of the anxiety lest he should say something wrong. Think of the possibility of his mind going a complete blank. Of course we all know the type that wants a chair and a glass of water. Then we're all of us, I think, pretty humane, whether the witness is putting on an act or not. But it's when there's no chair or glass of water asked for that we don't always realize the strain the witness may be undergoing. It must be a very alarming experience to give evidence in Court for the first time, even if you've nothing to gain or lose by the case. But I was telling you about when I gave evidence. It was about a compromise. I was called to prove that there had been a compromise or was it the other way about? But, wait a moment, what was it you were asking me?'

Roger repeated his problem.

'I see,' said Mr Justice Pantin. 'I'm sorry. I'm afraid I do tend to run on. But, oddly enough, not, I think, in my judgements. I'm rather like an actor with St Vitus' dance who can control it when he's on the stage but never when he's off. Which reminds me. Did you ever see – now, there I go. I'll try and control it this time. Yes, I see your difficulty. There's a lot to be said for altering the form of oath. But there still are people who are affected by the solemnity of the words. The invocation of the Almighty still influences some people. Not just the fear of a prosecution for perjury, but the fact that they are swearing by God. But for a lot of people it would be just as good to say "I promise to tell the truth". They'd tell as much truth after that – or as little – as they would after the present form. But that doesn't help you with your case. Of course a lot of us would just pack him off to Brixton until he became a little less refined in his ideas. But I agree with you – it's worth taking a lot of trouble to avoid that. Let me think.' The old man thought for about a minute. 'If I were you,' he said, 'I'd point out again that the words "the truth, the whole truth", etc., can only mean "what I believe to be the truth". Tell him he's quite right in saying that none of us know the truth for absolute certainty about anything and that you take the responsibility of telling him as a judge that the words he says are not to be interpreted literally.'

'And suppose he falls back on his objection to swearing at all?'

'Let your yea be yea and your nay, nay,' said Mr Justice Pantin. 'Yes – well, if he says that, I should let him affirm.'

'I've told him he may do that.'

'Well, tell him again,' said Mr Justice Pantin. 'That deals with one of his troubles. But if he won't swear and he won't affirm, well, in the end you'll have to send him off to Brixton. But with your persuasive manner I'm sure you'll win.'

Roger thanked his adviser and, after a further chat about other matters, he went back to court. Mr Jones came into the witness box. Roger began: 'Now, Mr Jones, I've been thinking over what you've said to me – '

'My Lord,' began counsel for the defendant. Mr Steaming was a rather irritating counsel. He was inclined to interrupt the judge and hardly ever for any good reason. During the course of the case Roger had suffered him fairly patiently, but he had had at last to ask him to refrain from interrupting.

'Mr Steaming,' said Roger, 'it must be obvious to you that this witness is causing considerable difficulty. I shall be obliged if you will wait until I have finished.'

'But, my Lord, I thought – ' went on Mr Steaming.

'Really,' said Roger. 'This is too bad. I am, I hope, being as patient as possible, but it's difficult enough to make this witness understand the right point of view without interruption. It is impossible with.'

'I only wanted to say, my Lord – ' said Mr Steaming.

'I dare say you did, Mr Steaming,' said Roger, now thoroughly irritated, 'but why can't it wait?'

'Because, my Lord,' said Mr Steaming, 'I only wanted to say I'd called Mr Jones by accident. I don't really want him as a witness at all.'

CHAPTER SIXTEEN

The Jungle

Roger had always remembered the first time his voice was heard in Court. That was one advantage of being appointed a judge so young; his early days were not so long ago. So he was particularly sympathetic towards young men who had been left behind by their masters to hold the fort. Whenever possible, he would accede to such an application as: 'Would your Lordship allow the cross-examination of this witness to stand over until my learned friend Mr Snail returns?'

But on one occasion the application was so fiercely opposed by counsel on the other side that Roger felt he must refuse it.

'B-but,' began the young man. 'I d-don't know what to ask.'

'Never mind,' said Roger. 'Suppose I suggest something to begin with.'

'That's very g-good of your Lordship.'

So Roger started the young man's cross-examination, and was soon making such progress that counsel on the other side began to wish devoutly that he had agreed to wait till the young man's master returned.

Indeed, eventually he said: 'My Lord, if your Lordship will forgive me, I think I was perhaps rather hasty and unfair to my learned friend when I said that I didn't agree for his cross-examination to stand over. If your Lordship will allow me, I should now like to accede to his application.'

'Now, I wonder,' said Roger, 'why you've changed your mind. I'm not asking too many questions myself, am I, by any chance?'

'Oh – no, my Lord,' said counsel, 'it was just that I felt it might be better if the cross-examination stood over.'

'What do you say, Mr Purse?' said Roger to the young man. 'Now that you're warming to it, would you like to go on or not?'

'I think perhaps my learned leader would prefer – my Lord – '

'Very well,' said Roger. 'As you ask me and as your application is no longer opposed, I might say, is now supported by your ever considerate opponent, I'll agree to it.'

There was a pretty girl sitting in the back of the court. Roger wondered if it was the young man's sister or girl friend. He remembered how once – but he must get on with the case in hand, not reminisce to himself now.

One morning Roger had experience of a new type of counsel. Mr Meldon had only recently been called to the Bar but he was a little over thirty. It very soon became apparent that, before being a barrister, he had been a high-pressure salesman, and he obviously thought that there was no reason why he should not make good use of his past experience in presenting his cases. After all, he had worn down hard-headed business men and cautious housewives, why not judges too?

'My Lord,' he began in opening his case to Roger. 'This is a claim which will cause your Lordship no difficulty at all. Of that I can assure your Lordship. I have two witnesses who will only have to be seen to be believed. They are both persons of the strictest integrity and their memories are extremely good. Your Lordship will be able to rely with confidence on every word they say.'

'Hardly worth fighting the case,' murmured his opponent to a neighbour.

'I've no doubt,' said Mr Meldon, 'that my learned friend thinks that he has some very good witnesses too, but the proof of the pudding is, if I may say so, my Lord, in the eating, and your Lordship will find, when you compare the witnesses on each side, that those called on behalf of the plaintiff are very much superior to those called on behalf of the defendant.'

Roger could not resist intervening with: 'Do you mean to look at, Mr Meldon?'

Nothing daunted, Mr Meldon replied: 'In appearance, learning, diction and last but by no means least, I hope, my Lord, in honesty.'

'What are their vital statistics?' whispered his opponent but loud enough to be heard.

Mr Meldon ignored the interruption.

'Wouldn't it be better if you told me something about the case, Mr Meldon, rather than enlarge on the beauties of your witnesses?' said Roger.

'Yes, indeed, my Lord, I was coming to the case. Now your Lordship has in the past tried numerous cases on various subjects. Some of the cases have been plain, some fairly plain, and some far from plain. But I venture to say to your Lordship that this case that I am presenting to your Lordship is the plainest case that your Lordship has ever tried. Plain, if I may say so, beyond a peradventure.'

'You may not say so,' said Roger gently.

'I beg your Lordship's pardon,' said the puzzled Mr Meldon, who was not used to the customer intervening at this early stage.

'Your duty and your only right', said Roger, 'is to make submissions to the Court. You are not allowed to give me the benefit of your own opinion, however valuable.'

'If your Lordship pleases,' said Mr Meldon slightly abashed and completely unaware of the respect in which he had offended. However, he soon recovered.

'Well, my Lord,' he said, 'your Lordship will find that the plaintiff is entitled to succeed in this case beyond any doubt of any kind whatsoever.'

'Wouldn't it be more helpful, from your point of view, in order to arrive at that desirable result, to tell me what the case is about?' said Roger.

'Of course, my Lord. I shall, of course, do so, but at the moment I am trying to condition your Lordship.'

Roger had read of people biting their lips until the blood came, and he now for the first time realized that it might actually happen. But he had to keep on biting for some time.

'That's very kind of you, Mr Meldon,' he said eventually, 'but normally in these courts counsel opening a case tells the judge what it is about before he does anything else.'

'Thank you, my Lord,' said Mr Meldon. 'Then the pep talk comes later?'

Roger nearly drew blood again.

'Suppose you tell me what the claim is for,' he said, as soon as he was able to speak.

'Certainly, my Lord. My clients who are reputable members of a reputable trade sold the defendant a motor car.'

'What is their trade, Mr Meldon?' asked Roger.

Mr Meldon looked puzzled.

'I've just told your Lordship,' he said, 'the motor car trade.'

'Thank you,' said Roger. 'I see.'

'The car was, I need hardly say, in perfect condition, and had only been registered the previous year. A new car of the same make would have cost a thousand pounds. My clients only charged three hundred and fifty pounds.'

'Are they a benevolent institution?' said Roger; 'three hundred and fifty pounds for a thousand-pound car?'

'I'm glad your Lordship has noticed that,' said Mr Meldon. 'That's a point I want to bring out. My clients' business has always been conducted on those lines, a very small margin of profit so as to have a quick turnover and an ever-increasing goodwill. If your Lordship went to my clients' showrooms – '

'I don't think,' said Roger, 'this is the time or place to try to sell me one of their cars.'

'Oh – my Lord,' said Mr Meldon. 'I shouldn't dream of doing any such thing, though if I may say so, your Lordship could go further and fare worse.'

'Never mind where I'm going,' said Roger. 'What about this car that the plaintiff sold to the defendant? Didn't it go? Did the plaintiff pay for it? What are your clients now suing for?'

'Ah, my Lord,' said Mr Meldon. 'I can well understand that your Lordship is impatient to hear the details. But they will be no worse for being waited for. What's good keeps, my Lord.'

'Mr Meldon,' said Roger firmly but still kindly, 'you have not been very long at the Bar and I think you'll find things easier if you take a hint from the Bench now and then and do what the judge asks you to do.'

'My Lord, I shall be delighted,' said Mr Meldon. 'It is not as though my clients have anything to hide or anything to be ashamed of. They have, as I've told your Lordship, an unanswerable case.'

'Well, please let me hear it,' said Roger. 'What are you suing for?'

'Your Lordship will already have seen,' began Mr Meldon.

'Mr Meldon, I'm sorry to keep on interrupting you, but I have seen nothing so far,' said Roger. 'I never look at the pleadings until I am referred to them by counsel. And I'm bound to say I'm beginning to doubt if we will ever reach that stage.'

'Oh, we will indeed, my Lord, and your Lordship will find the pleadings very rich, very rich indeed.'

Roger sighed and waited.

'Now, my Lord, the defendant took away the car – would he have done that if he had not been satisfied? – and he gave the plaintiff a cheque, and, my Lord, I have the cheque here. It is present in court and I'm going to make it an exhibit.'

Mr Meldon paused in order to get what he considered the right dramatic effect. He was leading up to his climax.

'My Lord,' he said in a somewhat hushed voice, 'that cheque – that cheque was – was – *dishonoured*.'

Mr Meldon stopped, as though waiting for applause. After a moment Roger said, in a very matter-of-fact voice: 'So you're suing on the dishonoured cheque? Is that the case?'

'My Lord,' said Mr Meldon, feeling that Roger had not appreciated the full force of his words, 'the cheque was *dishonoured*.'

'So I assume,' said Roger. 'Your clients couldn't have sued on it, if it had been paid.'

'Nor would they have done so,' said Mr Meldon. 'That is not the way they carry on their business.'

Roger had recourse to his lip again and, when he had recovered, he asked: 'Why was the cheque dishonoured?'

'Your Lordship may well ask,' said Mr Meldon.

'Well, I do ask,' said Roger, 'and I should really like to know the answer.'

'My Lord,' said Mr Meldon, 'I hold in my hand the cheque. It is signed by the defendant. It was *dishonoured* by the defendant,' and he held up the cheque in his hand.

'Yes, you've told me all that. Why was it dishonoured?'

'Because, my Lord,' said Mr Meldon, 'because the defendant has the impudence to say that it was obtained by fraud.'

'I see,' said Roger.

'In order to evade his just liabilities the defendant does not scruple to make this wicked allegation against my highly respectable clients. They have come to meet this charge and I venture to say to your Lordship, that that charge will be found to be as worthless as is apparently the defendant's signature on the cheque.'

'What is the alleged fraud?' asked Roger.

'The defendant says that this car was manufactured twenty years ago.'

'Well, was it?' asked Roger.

'Some very good cars indeed were manufactured twenty years ago,' said Mr Meldon. 'Indeed some people in the trade think that the quality of those cars is superior to many which are being made today.'

'I dare say,' said Roger, 'but do I gather from that, that you admit that the car was in fact manufactured twenty years ago?'

'Yes, that is quite correct, my Lord.'

'I think I see now what the case is going to be about. The defendant says that your clients represented that the car was made last year, whereas, in fact, it was made twenty years ago. Is that right, Mr Meldon?'

'That is, indeed, what the defendants say, my Lord, but what in fact happened is that my clients said that the car was first *registered* last year. They said nothing as to when it was manufactured.'

'So that's the issue, is it?' said Roger. 'Tell me, what happened to the car between its manufacture and its first registration?'

'It was used in the Army, my Lord, and then sold by auction by the Ministry of Supply. I need hardly tell your Lordship of the care with which the car was likely to be used when being driven in the Army. It was a *Commanding Officer's* car, my Lord. I need say no more.'

'Good,' said Mr Meldon's opponent under his breath.

'Why didn't the registration book show that the car, although first registered last year, was ex-Army stock?'

'My Lord, I'm instructed that registration books should show the fact, but they do not always do so.'

'I see,' said Roger. 'So that, if one's buying a second-hand car, the date of the first registration does not necessarily mean that the car was new on that date?'

'Usually it does, my Lord, but not always.'

'Well, if this case does nothing else,' said Roger, 'I hope it will put the public on their guard about that matter. I suppose the actual date of manufacture can easily be ascertained by looking at the engine or chassis number?'

'Yes, my Lord. Most dealers have a book which shows them the year of manufacture for one or other of those numbers.'

'So your clients knew that the car was an old one?'

'Yes, my Lord.'

'Did they tell that to the defendant?'

'Oh, my Lord,' said Mr Meldon with a deprecating gesture of his hands, 'the vendor need not decry his own goods, need he?'

'But I thought you said that the car might be all the better for being made twenty years ago,' said Roger.

'Ah, my Lord,' said Mr Meldon virtuously, 'my clients are not the sort of people to take advantage of a point like that.'

'So the long and short of it is,' said Roger, 'that your clients told the defendant that the car was first registered last year, that the defendant thought that meant the car was one year old and that when he found it wasn't, be claimed that he had been tricked.'

'Yes, my Lord,' said Mr Meldon. 'Absurd isn't it?'

'I don't see anything absurd in it,' said Roger.

'But, my Lord, look at the price my clients charged. The defendant couldn't have expected a nearly new car for that.'

'Well, Mr Meldon,' said Roger, 'you yourself pointed out to me that your clients prided themselves on making a very low margin of profit. May they not have said that to the defendant?'

'If they did, my Lord, it was true.'

'I dare say, but that may have satisfied the defendant's curiosity as to why such a low price was charged for such a new car.'

'Anyway, my Lord, it was a very good car. The defendant drove away in it himself.'

'That was something,' said Roger. 'Did he by any chance ring up shortly afterwards and say the car had broken down?'

Mr Meldon looked astonished.

'My Lord,' he said in a surprised tone. 'How did your Lordship know?'

'I didn't,' said Roger, 'but I have had some experience of these cases.'

'But that, of course, has nothing to do with it, my Lord. A car has to break down some time. And, after all, this one was twenty years old. We must all break down some time, my Lord.'

'Whenever we were first registered,' said Roger.

Eventually the plaintiff's counsel was prevailed upon by Roger to produce his beautiful witnesses. Before he did so, Roger asked Mr Meldon's opponent, Mr Brent, whether it wasn't really for the defendant to call his evidence first, in view of the fact that the drawing and dishonouring of the cheque were admitted.

'Yes, my Lord,' said Mr Brent, 'your Lordship is, of course, right. I may tell your Lordship, though, that I mentioned this to my learned friend before he opened the case. Whereupon he said he wanted to tell the judge what the plaintiff's case was. I then said that, if he opened the case, he'd have to call his witnesses first. He said that that was what he had every intention of doing. He then started to describe the beauty of his witnesses, but I was in a better position to duck than your Lordship.'

'Very well,' said Roger.

So Mr Meldon called his witnesses. First he called a typical car salesman with an Air Force moustache, and a spurious Oxford-BBC-Guards accent. Among other questions Mr Meldon asked him: 'Tell me, Mr Plaster, have you ever in the course of your career described a car to a customer in language which was not entirely justified?'

'Good Heavens, no, sir,' was the reply. 'I wouldn't keep my job for a moment if I did.'

'Are the cars you sell always worth what the customer pays for them or more?'

'Oh, certainly, sir. I'd be prepared to swear to that.'

'You are swearing to it,' said Roger.

'Quite, my Lord.'

'And it's true?' asked Roger.

'Oh, yes, my Lord.'

'That you've never sold a customer a car which was not worth what he paid for it?'

'Well, my Lord, there may have been something wrong with the car which I didn't know about.'

'And have customers sometimes complained that there was something wrong with cars you have sold them?'

'Oh, my Lord, customers are always complaining. Most of them don't understand cars,' said the witness.

'That must make it much easier to sell cars to them,' said Roger.

'Oh, no, my Lord,' said the witness. 'Much harder. They can't see what bargains they are getting.'

Later Mr Meldon called his second witness, a Mr Prince. He was of a very different order.

'Look,' he said in cross-examination, 'the car trade is rather like driving in London. Each man for himself and no quarter asked or given. It's a jungle.'

'And what particular animal are you?' asked Mr Brent.

'It all depends,' said Mr Prince. 'At the moment I'd like to be a monkey, safe up in the trees and throwing nuts at you.'

'And how would you describe yourself when you're selling a car? A snake? A crocodile?'

'No, sir, thank you. I do very well as I am. Homo sap something, I think they call it. I don't know where the sap comes in.'

'He comes into your showrooms, doesn't he?'

Mr Prince smiled.

'Yes, sir. Not one every minute, as I should like,' he said, 'but enough to give me an honest living.'

'An honest living?' queried Mr Brent. 'You'd say anything, wouldn't you, to sell a car?'

'To tell you the truth, sir, words don't mean a thing. When I buy a car, I go by the car, not by what's said about it.'

'Quite, Mr Prince, but people outside the trade are not so fortunate. They don't know what to look for.'

'And if they did,' volunteered Mr Prince, 'they mightn't find it, I can tell you.'

'You're being very frank,' said Roger. 'Why?'

'Well, my Lord,' said Mr Prince, 'I've sworn to tell the truth, and it's a new experience.'

'You like it then?' asked Roger.

'I like it here all right,' said the witness, 'but it wouldn't be any good in my business. Go broke in no time.'

'Well, Mr Prince,' said Roger, 'it's very refreshing to hear so frank a witness. Perhaps you can help me over this case. It's going to be said by the defendant that he was told this car was manufactured about a year ago. Did you tell him that?'

'It wasn't necessary, my Lord. We couldn't keep him off the car. You see, my Lord, we advertised it as "first registered last year." And so it was. Then we put: "New price £1,000. Our price £350." It would have been cruelty not to sell him the car. He'd set his heart on it.'

'Did he ask why it was being sold so cheaply?'

'I expect so, my Lord. They usually do.'

'And what was he told?' asked Mr Brent.

'The usual, I expect, but I don't remember exactly. Have too many cases like this.'

'By "the usual" you mean that you worked on small profits and quick returns?'

'That's right.'

'But that wasn't a true answer, was it?' asked Roger. 'The car was being sold at that price because it was a very old car.'

'Well the price was worked out by what we'd paid for it, and, as a matter of fact, it's quite true we do work on a very small margin of profit. If we can make five pounds over a car quick, it's better than waiting to make ten pounds. That's the way we look at it.'

'So that, when you tell customers that you work on a low margin of profit, that's actually true?' said Roger.

'Yes, so it is, my Lord,' said Mr Prince, slightly surprised. 'Now, I'm not saying that's why we say it, my Lord, but it just happens that way. Rather like in driving. Every now and then a taxi-driver says "after you". But that's when he hasn't a fare and wants to dawdle.'

The case went on and Roger eventually decided that the defendant had been told not simply that the car had been registered the year before but that it had been made the year before. So he found against the plaintiffs. Mr Meldon had failed to make a sale.

Outside the court he offered his sympathy to Mr Prince.

'Oh, that's all right, old chap,' said Mr Prince, 'you did your best, but it's the same here as in the trade. It doesn't pay to tell the truth. I'll know better another time. I couldn't sell you a new Vauxhall, second-hand, could I, first registered next year?'

CHAPTER SEVENTEEN

The Trojan Kitchen

From time to time a High Court Judge is asked to sit in the Court of Appeal, when, for example, one of the Lords Justices is ill or performing some other duty, and it was not long before Roger was asked to do this. He sat with Lords Justices Crewe and Soulsby and they heard appeals from County Courts.

One of the first of these was an appeal from Henry and, for a moment, Roger felt a little odd at the thought. Roger, although not Henry's pupil, had probably learned more from Henry in his early days than from anyone else. And now here he was in a position to say: 'With the greatest respect to the learned judge, although his language is far from clear, I cannot think that he meant that.'

However, he soon got used to the idea and, as it turned out, he never had to use such an expression about any part of Henry's judgement.

The case had arisen as a result of trouble between a landlord and a tenant. Although, no doubt, practitioners in the County Court see many such cases, it is remarkable how comparatively few there are. After all, for many people it is difficult not to be, if not irritated, at the least inconvenienced by the footsteps, wireless noises, parties, and babies of the friends who live upstairs. If they are not friends, the irritation and inconvenience must be far worse, and, if they are on the worst possible terms with their downstairs neighbours, it is difficult to know how the latter can bear it and keep their sanity.

But they do. Up and down the country they manage to live somehow, without recourse to the Courts or nervous breakdowns. It is only a very small percentage of cases which find their way to the Courts, but every Court where the housing situation is acute (and this applies to most Courts) has a fair number of them.

The case which eventually came before Judge Blagrove and then before the Court of Appeal arose in this way. Mr Stream was the tenant of a small house with two floors and he had lived there for many years with his wife and growing family. When the children grew up and left to get married, the house seemed rather big for them and, with the permission of his landlord, Mr Stream sublet the upper floor to Mr and Mrs Bulge. The Bulges were very anxious to find a place and, although Mr Stream was unable to give them a proper kitchen, it was agreed that they should make do with a sort of kitchenette which Mr Bulge constructed on the upper landing. It was also agreed that the bathroom and lavatory should be shared by the two families.

Things went very well at first and Mr Stream found the Bulges' rent quite useful. But one day there was some altercation between Mrs Bulge and Mrs Stream which, though unimportant in itself, was the origin of the trouble. Within a week of this episode each side was asking the other to turn its wireless down. Within a month Mrs Stream was asking Mrs Bulge to walk more quietly up the stairs. Within two or three months it was difficult for the Bulges to move about upstairs without Mr or Mrs Stream banging with a broom on their ceiling. This was answered by the Bulges with deliberate thumps.

It was six months before the police had to be called the first time. Things were quieter for a few weeks after that, but then one evening, both sides, having consumed a certain amount of alcohol, a quantity which ordinarily would have made the parties mellow and happily ready for bed, happened to arrive home at the same time. They glared at each other and then Mr and Mrs Bulge, after thumping up the stairs, turned on their wireless.

Mr Stream shouted up to Mr Bulge to turn the wireless down. Mr Bulge asked Mr Stream if he'd like to come up and do it himself, and eventually, after a few further pleasantries, hostilities began. The police were called again.

After quiet had been restored the policeman asked what it was all about, whereupon both sides started to explain at once.

'Just a moment,' said the policeman, 'I think I'd better see you separately.'

'It'll be all lies she tells you,' volunteered Mrs Bulge.

'That's all right,' said the policeman, 'I'll listen to yours afterwards – your story, I mean.'

So the policeman interviewed Mr and Mrs Stream first. 'Well – they had the wireless on loud, so I asked them quite friendly to turn it up – '

'Down, you mean,' put in the policeman.

'Just a manner of speaking – and he threatened to murder me. I'd like to see him try. He hasn't the guts.'

'Then you weren't frightened he'll really try?'

'I'd like to see him, I could hit him if he did, couldn't I? That'd be self defence.'

'I shouldn't get mixed up in a fight,' said the policeman, 'you never know where it's going to end.'

'Well – what can we do? We can't stand any more of this.'

'Well,' said the policeman, 'if I were you I'd see a solicitor. Mind you, I'm not saying it'll be any good, but, if they really are a nuisance, you might be able to get an order for possession against them. But I can't tell you if you will. That's up to the lawyers.'

'D'you know one?'

'Well,' said the policeman, 'there's a chap called Digby opposite the police station. Quite a good chap and he won't skin you, like some of them. I'd go and see him.'

After a little further talk, the policeman went up to the Bulges and heard their side of the story.

'It's nag, nag, nag all the time. We don't get any peace at all,' said Mrs Bulge.

'They even pinch our letters,' said Mr Bulge.

'Ah,' said the policeman. 'That's bad, if you can prove it, but can you?'

'Well, we haven't seen them at it. They're too cunning for that. But how is it there's no letter when I go down in the morning, and half an hour later there's one on the mat? It can't grow there, though from the way they live downstairs I shouldn't be surprised if something started to grow there.'

'Well – what happened tonight?'

'Well, they started screaming and shouting, and if you hadn't come,' said Mr Bulge meaningly, 'I think someone might have got hurt.'

'Well, I shouldn't get mixed up in a fight,' advised the policeman. 'Don't start anything you can't finish is our motto at the station.'

'Well, what about the letters? There must be a law about that.'

'Well, if I were you, I should consult a solicitor about it. There's one just round the corner from the police station in Flint Street – name of Bromley.'

'Come to think, there's one opposite the police station, isn't there?' said Mr Bulge.

'Yes, there is,' said the policeman slowly, 'but if I were you I'd go to the one in Flint Street – Mr Digby's a bit busy at the moment. Now d'you think I can go back to the station without being called out again?'

'It's not our fault,' said Mrs Bulge. 'We keep ourselves to ourselves.'

'I know, mum, just how it is,' said the policeman, and went back to the station.

The next day the Streams consulted Mr Digby, who listened to them courteously and at length. In consequence a summons was issued in the Pendlebury County Court for possession of the Bulges' rooms on the ground of nuisance. The details were long and varied.

1. Threatening to murder Mr Stream.
2. Using abusive and obscene language towards Mr and Mrs Stream.
3. Deliberately playing the wireless too loud late at night.
4. Banging doors.
5. Deliberately hammering on the floor.
6. Moving furniture late at night.
7. Cutting the washing line in the garden just after Mrs Stream had put her washing out.
8. Taking the Streams' milk.
9. Assault.
10. Leaving the front door open.
11. Slamming the front door.
12. Preventing the Streams from using the lavatory.

As soon as the Bulges received the summons they went round to Mr Bromley. He was a quiet, modest little man who did not like appearing in Court, and invariably instructed counsel if it were possible. On this occasion he arranged that Mr and Mrs Bulge should have what he called the advantage of being represented by a young man called Docket. Mr Docket's enthusiasm considerably outweighed his experience, but he had the necessary wig, robes, and voice to appear in the Pendlebury County Court, and he was able to pay the fare there.

The day of the hearing arrived and Mr Docket made the journey from London by train. In the train he read his brief over again, and made more marks on it, underlining this passage, noting a query here and there, and generally putting the finishing touches to his work, like an artist with a picture. By the time he arrived at the Court everything was ready for an impassioned assault upon the Streams.

In the robing room he met Mr Digby, his opponent. Mr Digby was a solicitor of many years' experience who did a great deal of advocacy himself. He was known as the local Solicitor-General. After they had had a chat for a few minutes, Mr Docket expressed the view that he was sorry for anyone whose case was in the list after theirs. Mr Digby asked him why.

'Why?' said Mr Docket, in a surprised tone. 'Why? Because we'll take three hours at least, probably all day. Lucky we're at the head of the list.'

'D'you know why we're so high in the list?' said Mr Digby.

'A mistake, I suppose.'

'Not at all. D'you know this judge?'

'I can't say that I do,' said Mr Docket. 'What's he like?'

'Very nice, but he has a way with nuisance cases.'

'What d'you mean?' asked Mr Docket.

'Shall I tell you exactly what'll happen in our case?'

'If you can do so without giving away professional secrets, I'd be most grateful.'

'No secrets at all. You'll see for yourself in a moment. Our case is where it is because the clerk thinks it'll take about five minutes.'

'Five minutes!' said Mr Docket. 'It'll take you half an hour to open it, I should have thought.'

'So?' said Mr Digby. 'Shall I go on?'

'Well?' said Mr Docket.

'After I've opened the case for about two of your thirty minutes, the old boy will say: "Mr Docket and Mr Digby – don't you think this is the sort of case where the parties might put their heads together?" What he means by this is that the parties should have their heads banged together. I quite agree with him as a matter of fact.'

'Well, I don't,' said Mr Docket with some heat. 'I think your clients have behaved disgracefully, if my instructions are right.'

'My dear boy,' said Mr Digby, 'if you'll forgive my relying on my superiority in age and forgetting my inferiority in profession, don't be angry with me. If my instructions are right, your clients ought to be turned out of the house tomorrow.'

'I quite agree with you, if they're right. But, by the time I've cross-examined your Mr Stream, I fancy you won't be so sure of your client's instructions.'

'I'm afraid it doesn't require your cross-examination to produce that effect. In this sort of case it's very rare for either side to have correct instructions. But I was telling you what will happen – shall I go on?'

'Please.'

'Well, whatever either of us says – unless there's something really serious or unusual – he'll suggest an adjournment – "Just to see how things go on. Would you like me to say a word to each of your clients?" ' went on Mr Digby, giving a very good imitation of Henry's manner and voice. ' "Certainly. Now, Mr and Mrs Stream – Mr and Mrs Bulge – you each of you have my deepest sympathy in having to live with people you don't like. But in these days of housing shortage we just have to make the best of these things. Now, you both go away and try to see the good in each other. Of course if things don't improve, Mr Bulge, I may have to make an order against you or, if it's your fault, Mr Stream, I may have to dismiss the action with costs. Expensive business, going to law. Counsel and solicitors have to be paid, you know." '

'Does he always go on like that?' asked Mr Docket.

'Nearly always in nuisance cases on the first hearing. Of course, if it comes back to him he tries it.'

'Well, I'm going to make him try it today.'

'Go ahead, my dear boy,' said Mr Digby, 'I like to see enthusiasm.'

Soon afterwards, the case was called on and Mr Digby had not been speaking for more than a few minutes when the judge duly interrupted, and the next dialogue was as follows:

HENRY: Mr Digby, I've been looking at the allegations in this action. Don't you and Mr – er – Mr Docket think this is perhaps a case where you might put your heads together?

DIGBY: I should be very happy to take instructions on the point, your Honour.

HENRY: And you, Mr Docket?

DOCKET: My clients want the action heard today, your Honour.

HENRY: Quite so, Mr Docket, quite so. But have they considered the possibilities? Of course, I'm not expressing an opinion one way or the other – I don't know anything about the case – but, if I were satisfied – I say if I were satisfied that, for instance, your client had without sufficient provocation threatened to murder the plaintiff, I should take a very grave view of the matter.

DOCKET: My clients have a perfect explanation of that matter, your Honour.

HENRY: Quite so, Mr Docket, quite so – but just suppose for a moment that I don't accept that explanation – I'm not expressing any view at present naturally – I don't know who's in the right – though in this type of case it is not uncommon for it to be six of one and half a dozen of the other – suppose I don't accept the explanation – it would be most awkward for your clients if I made an order against them. They haven't anything to lose by an adjournment. If the plaintiff doesn't mind, I don't see why your clients should.

DOCKET: There are the letters, your Honour.

HENRY: Oh – your counterclaim. How many letters do your clients have in a week?

DOCKET: I'm not sure, your Honour.

HENRY: I rather suspect they don't have enough to make it worthwhile risking having an order for possession made against them. Surely with a little goodwill on both sides something can be arranged and we can see how things go?

DOCKET: (*doggedly*): I should prefer to have the action tried, your Honour.

HENRY: Very well, then, Mr Docket. No doubt you have your instructions and must abide by them. Call your evidence, Mr Digby.

So the case proceeded, and after two and a half hours Henry gave judgement as follows:

'It is a great pity', he said, 'that my advice was not accepted two and a half hours ago. There is nothing whatever to choose between either of the parties, as I rather suspected from the start. Both claim and counterclaim will be dismissed, and each side will bear its own costs.'

But it was not from that decision that the case went to the Court of Appeal. Mr and Mrs Stream went home very unhappily, and, as soon as it was opening time, Mr Stream went out to drown his sorrows. In the public house he met a solicitor's clerk. They got talking and Mr Stream confided his troubles to the stranger. Over the third pint, Mr Stream was given some advice which he decided to act upon as soon as possible.

He went home and told his wife about it. The next thing that happened was that the Bulges came home triumphant, banged their way up the stairs and turned the radio on. After all, they had only lost their claim about their letters. The real fight they had won. As they did not receive the usual response to the noise they were making, Mr Bulge came out on the landing and, pretending to hear some noise from below, shouted down: 'Stop that ruddy noise, will you?'

He could only just be heard above the blaring of their own radio, and Mr Bulge thought he must have misheard the reply that seemed to come from below. For what Mr Stream had in fact said was: 'Sorry, old man.'

Quite certain that he was mistaken, Mr Bulge yelled down even louder: 'Stop that ruddy noise.'

But this time there was no doubt about the reply, because Mr Stream came out of his room and, instead of the usual expletives, he said: 'So sorry, old man.'

Mr Bulge was very much taken aback. The only reply he could think of was: 'Well, do something about it then,' and he went back to his own room, and grumbled even more than usual about the people down below.

But the next morning, which was a Sunday, there was another surprise for the Bulges. About noon there was a knock on the door and there was Mr Stream. Mr Bulge said aggressively: 'What d'you want?'

'I only came up about the noise last night,' began Mr Stream apologetically.

'We'll make as much noise as we ruddy well like,' said Bulge. 'Take us to Court, would you?'

'No,' said Mr Stream, with unaccustomed mildness, 'you've got me wrong. I wanted to say I was sorry about the noise *we* were making. To tell you the truth, I was in a bit of a two and eight. Lucky not to have been picked up by the old grasshopper.'

Mr Bulge was so surprised that he could only say: 'Oh!' And then added grudgingly, rather like a judge granting an adjournment which it is personally inconvenient for him to grant: 'Very well.'

Mr Stream went away and Mr Bulge asked his wife whether she thought Mr Stream was going round the bend. If she did, there was confirmation for her view during the next fortnight. For whatever the Bulges did or said the Streams behaved with an incredible meekness, and started to go out of their way to try to do favours for the Bulges. It was not long before this method of attack had its effect, and the parties started to smile at each other when they met. And the Bulges no longer stamped up the stairs – they walked up them. One thing led to another and it was not long before they were having drinks together. After several sessions anyone who met them would have thought that they had always been bosom friends.

It was when the relationship had been pretty well cemented that one day Mr Stream made his finest gesture of all.

'It must be pretty awkward', he said, 'for your old woman cooking up on the landing. How would it be if you shared our kitchen? Of course, I'd have to ask the missus, but she and your missus seem to get along all right.'

'Well, that's very kind of you, old man,' said Mr Bulge, and spoke to his wife about it. Within a week it had been agreed that the rent should be increased by sixpence, and that the Bulges should share the Streams' kitchen.

Mrs Stream did find it a bit irksome after many years of having her own kitchen to share it with that – with the lady upstairs. But she controlled herself and made the best of it. So for at least two months after the new arrangement (which had been confirmed by the presentation to the Bulges, at the expense of the Streams, of a brand-new rent book) things went well. But after that time Mr and Mrs Stream started to make remarks to each other or to themselves which the Bulges could and were intended to hear. At first, in view of the new relationship, they thought they must have misheard and took no notice, but that could not go on for long. It only required one retort from Mrs Bulge to a sarcastic aside from Mrs Stream about the dirt that some people carried around with them, to set the smouldering embers ablaze. Once more the rows began, but, within a week from the first real one, Mr Stream had served on the Bulges a notice to quit.

'Here's what I think of that,' said Mr Bulge, and tore it up into little pieces and threw it down the stairs.

'You've had it anyway,' said Mr Stream.

'So have you,' said Mr Bulge. 'Take me to Court again! Don't make me laugh.'

But Mr Stream did take Mr Bulge to court again, and this time there was a difference, because the summons said nothing about noise or misbehaviour or anything as offensive as that. It was a mild little affair, the summons. Or so Mr Bulge thought, until he took it to his solicitor.

'Oh, dear,' said Mr Bromley, 'you have got yourself into a mess.'

'We ain't done nothing,' said Mr Bulge.

'Oh, but you have, Mr Bulge, you have indeed. You've made a new tenancy agreement with Mr Stream, under which you share the kitchen.'

'They suggested it,' said Mr Bulge.

'No doubt they did,' said Mr Bromley, 'no doubt they did. But you agreed to it, and, once you did that, you lost the protection of the Rent Act. You didn't know, I suppose, that a landlord who shares his kitchen with his tenant can get the tenant out, whenever he likes, if he gives him notice to quit?'

'The dirty – ' began Mr Bulge.

'I quite understand your feelings,' said Mr Bromley. 'It was a very dirty trick, but strong words are no good – we've got to see what we can do to get you out of it. I'll send the papers to counsel at once.'

In consequence Mr Docket again met Mr Digby at the Pendlebury County Court. When they first met in the robing room, Mr Docket gave the solicitor a very curt 'good morning'.

'It's nothing to do with me,' said Mr Digby, 'I never suggested it to them. They met a solicitor's clerk in a pub and he put them up to it. You say anything you like about it in Court. I quite agree with you. But how are you going to get out of it?'

'I say it's fraud,' said Mr Docket.

'I know you do in the defence,' said Mr Digby, 'but how are you going to prove it?'

'Well, if this isn't fraud, I don't know what is,' said Mr Docket.

However, Henry, after a patient hearing, decided that, although in a sense the Bulges had been tricked into making the new agreement, it did not amount to fraud in law, and regretfully he made an order for possession against the Bulges.

It was from that decision that the Bulges appealed, and Roger and the two Lords Justices had yet another case which dealt with the strange story of the shared kitchen. For strange it seems to some people that the Courts expressly, and Parliament impliedly, have decided that, as long as a landlord only shares a bathroom or a lavatory with a tenant, the tenant is fully protected by the Rent Acts. And, indeed, if he only has a partial use of the kitchen, such as for boiling water occasionally, he is still protected. But, once he has the right to use the kitchen equally with his landlord, he has apparently lost the protection of the Rent Acts. The exact principle upon which it has been decided that the sharing of a bath or a lavatory is different from the sharing of a kitchen is a little difficult for some people to follow, except, of course, that the bathroom and lavatory are not used at the same time by both landlord and tenant. But then, normally, neither is the gas stove or sink. However, that is the law, as the Bulges found to their cost, and there is no getting away from it. The only escape available to the Bulges was if they could show that they had, in the legal sense, been cheated into making the new agreement by which they shared the kitchen.

Mr Docket, who appeared for the Bulges, soon found that addressing the Court of Appeal was very different from appearing in a County Court. He had only just started when he received a fast ball from Lord Justice Crewe.

'But, Mr Docket,' he said, 'the judge has negatived fraud. Surely that's an end of the matter? It's purely a question of fact, isn't it?'

'I suppose,' said Roger, observing that Mr Docket did not seem in a condition to deal with the delivery, 'that you would say, Mr Docket, that the learned judge did say that the defendants had – to use his own words – been tricked into making the new agreement.'

'Yes, my Lord,' said Mr Docket eagerly, thankful to have found a friend so early.

'And you'd go on to say, I suppose,' said Roger, 'that, although the learned judge has negatived fraud, that decision is inconsistent with his finding that the defendants were tricked?'

'Yes, indeed, my Lord,' said Mr Docket.

'But,' said Lord Justice Crewe, looking at Mr Docket, but talking at Roger, 'the actual words of the learned judge were – "in a sense tricked" – were they not?'

'Yes, my Lord,' said Mr Docket less hopefully, and glancing towards Roger in the hope that he would find whatever was the best answer.

'Well, Mr Docket,' went on the Lord Justice, but this time actually looking at Roger, 'the learned judge plainly knew what are the ingredients necessary to prove fraud, and he came to the conclusion that they were not established.

Was he doing more in using the words you mention than saying in more elegant language that it was what might be termed colloquially "a dirty trick"?'

'Well, my Lord,' said Mr Docket, 'I submit – ' and he paused sufficiently long to show Roger that he had no idea what to submit.

'Yes, Mr Docket,' said Roger, 'you say, I suppose, that a learned judge of the experience and learning of Judge Blagrove, if I may say so, chooses his language carefully. He did not say that it was a dirty trick, but that the defendants had been tricked.'

'In a sense, Mr Docket,' put in Lord Justice Crewe.

'Yes, in a sense,' conceded Roger. 'But tricked. Tricked,' he repeated. 'And I'm bound to say that, for my part, I agree with the learned Judge. The defendants *were* tricked. The whole behaviour of the plaintiffs was a lie – an acted lie. Their pretence that they liked the defendants, for example, was not that as much a fraudulent representation as an ordinary deliberate lie? Is that what you say, Mr Docket?'

'Yes, indeed, my Lord,' said Mr Docket.

'But, Mr Docket, really,' said Lord Justice Crewe, 'can you rely on that? Was it in your defence?'

'Well, my Lord,' began Mr Docket unhappily, for it was not in his clients' written defence, but, before he could finish, Roger intervened with: 'But in the County Court it doesn't have to be, does it? You can rely on any defence at the trial, whatever may be in the written defence.'

Roger leaned across to Lord Justice Crewe: 'I believe it's Order 9 Rule 8,' he whispered.

'I dare say,' said Lord Justice Crewe testily. He did not expect a fairly new puisne judge to talk as much as Roger was talking.

'You were saying, Mr Docket,' went on Roger, 'that, if a man tells a lie, he can just as easily live a lie. A deaf and dumb man can tell a lie. A tic-tac man at a racecourse can certainly tell a lie with his hands. In this case it was not just the actions of the defendants. It was the words as well. Is it conceivable that Mrs Bulge would have agreed to have shared a kitchen with a person who disliked her? You say it isn't, Mr Docket?'

'Yes, my Lord, I do.'

'And you add, I suppose, that it was by pretending that they were reconciled and that the Streams really liked the Bulges, when the truth was that they intended to get them out of the house as soon as they could, that the plaintiffs tricked the defendants into making the new agreement? Why isn't that just as much fraud vitiating the new agreement as if they told some other lie about it? I fancy that, if the evidence were examined, a very large number of untruths told by the plaintiffs would emerge. Every time Mr and Mrs Stream made a conciliatory statement or gesture, it was untrue and it was made fraudulently.'

'What', said Lord Justice Crewe, 'did the learned judge say to that point, Mr Docket, when you put it to him – no doubt as forcefully as you are putting it to us?'

'He was against me, my Lord.'

'Yes, yes, we know that. But was it really put to him in the form you are now putting it to us? My brother Thursby was not able to lead you at the County Court.'

'My Lord, I did submit the whole thing was a fraud,' said Mr Docket.

'And presumably', said Roger, 'by "the whole thing" you must have meant the behaviour and language of the defendants from first to last?'

'Yes, my Lord,' said Mr Docket.

'And did the learned judge give any indication that he did not so understand it?'

'No, my Lord.'

'And did the learned judge,' said Lord Justice Crewe, 'give any indication that he did understand it in the way you are putting it to us?'

'Your answer to that, Mr Docket,' said Roger, 'is, I suppose, the use of the words "in a sense tricked". How, you ask, could the learned judge suppose that the defendants had in a sense been tricked unless it was because of the words and behaviour of the plaintiffs for the weeks preceding the new agreement?'

'Yes, that's what I say,' said Mr Docket.

Lord Justice Crewe leaned towards the other Lord Justice.

'You're very quiet,' he whispered. 'What's your view about it all?'

'I'm thinking,' replied Lord Justice Soulsby.

'Good exercise,' whispered Lord Justice Crewe, 'but what about? Forgive me,' he added aloud, and motioned to Roger to come and talk to him and the other Lord Justice. Roger got up and went and stood between his two senior brethren. They talked in undertones.

'Well, is Thursby right?' asked Lord Justice Crewe.

'I must say', said Lord Justice Soulsby, 'that Blagrove doesn't seem to have considered this point at all. He seems to have looked for some ordinary untrue statement before the new agreement, but he doesn't seem to have dealt with the possibility that the whole set-up – words and music – was untrue. I suppose he could have found that it was just a coincidence, and that the parties had genuinely got on better together.'

'He doesn't seem to have dealt with that aspect at all. Won't it have to go back for a new trial?'

Meanwhile, Mr Docket was being encouraged by the London agent of Mr Bromley, a Mr Marrow.

'Stick to it,' he said, 'you're doing fine.'

'Thank you,' said Mr Docket.

'Don't sit down till Thursby's said everything he can think of. He's making a jolly good judge. He'll be in the Court of Appeal in his own right soon, if he isn't careful.'

At this stage Roger went back to his own seat.

'We think', said Lord Justice Crewe, 'that in view of Mr Docket's powerful submission, we should like to hear what his opponent has to say.'

Eventually the appeal was allowed, the order for possession was set aside, and a new trial ordered – 'if', added Lord Justice Crewe, 'the parties really wish to continue this litigation. They have already had three hearings in Court. Might I suggest to their respective advisers that the parties might now try and forget the past, go back to the old arrangements of kitchens, and really try to behave as they did for a couple of months just before and just after the new arrangement was made. Whatever the truth about the case may be, we are all sure that the most certain chance of happiness lies in that direction, and not in a further hearing in the County Court with a possible further appeal to this court.'

'I don't see why he should have added that,' said Roger, when Henry and Sally next visited them. 'You wouldn't go wrong twice in the same case.'

'Thank you, Roger,' said Henry. 'You've always been such a comfort to me.'

'I hope you think we were right to upset you,' said Roger.

'Don't apologize,' said Henry, 'but, as a matter of fact, I do. It's an obvious point. Can't think how I missed it. Must be old age.'

At that moment the telephone rang. Roger answered it. It was Plummer.

'I've got some good news for you, old boy,' he said. 'D'you remember a boy called Barrow? We used to call him "Wheelbarrow".'

'Yes,' said Roger. 'He's an MP. What about him? And why is he good news?'

'Well, I've just heard that he's going to be the new Minister of Transport. So I'm going to help him make the wheels go round.'

'Poor fellow,' said Roger. 'Now I suppose you'll be leaving me alone.'

'Cross my heart,' said Plummer. 'That's if the papers are right. Anyway, I'm getting a bit tired of you. Have to be too careful. I think you're jolly good, by the way. A credit to the old school. Heard from Toni lately?'

'No,' said Roger, 'I haven't. Why d'you ask?'

'I just wondered,' said Plummer. 'Bye-bye. I've got to think up something to launch the new Minister.'

Roger reported the conversation to Henry, Sally, and Anne.

'I must say it's a bit of a relief,' he said, 'but after my first outing there wasn't much he could do.'

'What about Toni,' said Henry, 'you've never had to find her that doctor's job?'

'No,' said Roger, 'I'm afraid she's slipping out of our life.'

The telephone rang again.

'It's your turn, Anne,' said Roger.

Anne went to answer it and was back in a few moments. 'It's Toni,' she said. 'She wondered if you could introduce her to a doctor.'

'We've come just at the right moment,' said Henry. 'Shall we lock him up for you?' he asked Anne.

'It's very odd,' said Roger, as he went to the telephone.

'I do hope you don't mind my troubling you,' said Toni.

'No, of course not.'

'Well, you did say that, if I ever wanted a change, you might introduce me to a job as a doctor's receptionist.'

'Yes,' said Roger, 'I will, if you like.'

'That's very sweet of you,' said Toni. 'I'll tell you why it is. You see, I'm just going to get engaged.'

'My best wishes,' said Roger.

'And we – Charles and I – thought it would be better if I were described as a doctor's receptionist or something, rather than a dance hostess.'

'I see,' said Roger. 'Then it's only a very temporary job you want?'

'Oh very,' said Toni.

'Well please congratulate the lucky man for me,' said Roger.

'You know him,' said Toni. Roger hesitated for a moment.

'Do I?' he said.

'Yes, very well indeed.'

'You don't mean to say,' he began.

'I do,' said Toni. 'How will you like me as a sister in law? That would be a fair description, wouldn't it?'

After a little further conversation, Roger went back to the others.

'What d'you think?' he said, 'Toni's going to marry Charlie Breeze. She's a fast worker. I didn't even know they'd been seeing each other. She let Plummer think it was me.'

'A case,' said Henry, 'of a judge not manifestly being seen to be done.'

HENRY CECIL

ACCORDING TO THE EVIDENCE

Alec Morland is on trial for murder. He has tried to remedy the ineffectiveness of the law by taking matters into his own hands. Unfortunately for him, his alleged crime was not committed in immediate defence of others or of himself. In this fascinating murder trial you will not find out until the very end just how the law will interpret his actions. Will his defence be accepted or does a different fate await him?

THE ASKING PRICE

Ronald Holbrook is a fifty-seven-year-old bachelor who has lived in the same house for twenty years. Jane Doughty, the daughter of his next-door neighbours, is seventeen. She suddenly decides she is in love with Ronald and wants to marry him. Everyone is amused at first but then events take a disturbingly sinister turn and Ronald finds himself enmeshed in a potentially tragic situation.

> 'The secret of Mr Cecil's success lies in continuing to do superbly what everyone now knows he can do well.'
> – *The Sunday Times*

Henry Cecil

Brief Tales from the Bench

What does it feel like to be a Judge? Read these stories and you can almost feel you are looking at proceedings from the lofty position of the Bench.

With a collection of eccentric and amusing characters, Henry Cecil brings to life the trials in a County Court and exposes the complex and often contradictory workings of the English legal system.

'Immensely readable. His stories rely above all on one quality – an extraordinary, an arresting, a really staggering ingenuity.'
– *New Statesman*

Brothers in Law

Roger Thursby, aged twenty-four, is called to the bar. He is young, inexperienced and his love life is complicated. He blunders his way through a succession of comic adventures including his calamitous debut at the bar.

His career takes an upward turn when he is chosen to defend the caddish Alfred Green at the Old Bailey. In this first Roger Thursby novel Henry Cecil satirizes the legal profession with his usual wit and insight.

'Uproariously funny.' – *The Times*

'Full of charm and humour. I think it is the best Henry Cecil yet.' – P G Wodehouse

HENRY CECIL

HUNT THE SLIPPER

Harriet and Graham have been happily married for twenty years. One day Graham fails to return home and Harriet begins to realise she has been abandoned. This feeling is strengthened when she starts to receive monthly payments from an untraceable source. After five years on her own Harriet begins to see another man and divorces Graham on the grounds of his desertion. Then one evening Harriet returns home to find Graham sitting in a chair, casually reading a book. Her initial relief turns to anger and then to fear when she realises that if Graham's story is true, she may never trust his sanity again. This complex comedy thriller will grip your attention to the very last page.

THE WANTED MAN

When Norman Partridge moves to Little Bacon, a pretty country village, he proves to be a kind and helpful neighbour and is liked by everyone. Initially it didn't seem to matter that no one knew anything about his past or how he managed to live so comfortably without having to work.

Six months before, John Gladstone, a wealthy bank-robber had escaped from custody. Gradually, however, Partridge's neighbours begin to ask themselves questions. Was it mere coincidence that Norman Partridge had the build and features of the escaped convict? While some villagers are suspicious but reluctant to report their concerns to the police, others decide to take matters into their own hands...